Blessings
In
Hidden Places

1st Edition

Kristen Fox

A Blessing in Disguise

Dedicated to my amazing family. God blessed me when He put you three into my life. I've never spent a day alone in my fight because I have had an immeasurable amount of love and support from you three. Love you all more than you'll ever know!

DEAR JODY,

I PRAY THAT YOU CAN FIND ENCOURAGEMENT PEACE, & HOPE IN THE PAGES OF THE BOOK I PRAY THAT DISCOURAGEMENT SORROW & STRESS DO CREEP UP ON YOU. MAY GOD'S MERCY (NOT GETTING A PUNISHMENT WE DESERVE) & ~~MERCY~~ GRACE (GETTING A GIFT WE DONT DESERVE) SURROUNDS YOU! I ALSO PRAY YOURE ABLE TO FIND YOUR OWN BLESSINGS IN HIDDEN PLACES AS YOU NAVAGATE THIS LIFE!

♡, *[signature]*

Table of Contents

Forward

Contributions from my family.

Written by Tim Fox, my daddy.

You are in for a treat. I realize I may have a slightly biased opinion, but I hear and see this all the time from people that have the opportunity to interact with my daughter. I stopped by to see her at work last week and I was sitting in a chair in the central office area, where her desk is located, patiently waiting while she handled clients that needed her assistance. The United Parcel Service (UPS) delivery man stopped by the office just to give Kristen a hug. He had no packages to deliver, but in the few short months Kristen has worked at this establishment she has already had a major impact on this middle-aged African American. He calls her Sunshine. The clients in the office will ask me if I am her father and when I proudly say yes, they immediately pour on praise and gratitude for Kristen. Although it may seem like I am overstating Kristen's impact, I can assure you I am not.

Why does she affect people in this way? It is because she has a genuine concern for everyone's welfare and she wants to have a positive impact on every person's life. The UPS deliveryman has captured it in a single word...Sunshine. Her goal is bring hope, healing and yes, a little sunshine into every person she meets. Kristen's sincerity and concern for others are as natural to her as breathing is to you or me. However, this gift has been shaped and molded through the crucible of pain and suffering.

Kristen has suffered since childbirth from a chronic digestive disorder, which has steadily gotten worse as she has gotten older. This condition has caused her great physical pain, but it has also resulted in psychological and emotional pain as well. Can you imagine going through your adolescent and young adult years with a condition like this plaguing you on a daily basis? Some of you reading this book can relate because you are going through or have gone through your own personal 'wilderness' experience. If this describes your situation then this book will encourage you to "press on!" despite your obstacles or challenges. Maybe you haven't been through a valley as dark and dreary as described here, but you are still searching for significance and a meaning for your life. I have good news for you as well. This book will lead you to the One that can fill that void in your inner being. It will lead you to the Living Water that will quench your thirst for eternity. Kristen has found peace and rest in the arms of her Heavenly Father and through the redemptive work of Jesus Christ, who died and rose again for everyone…no matter what you have done or the pain and suffering you face. My prayer is that you too will leave your burden at the foot of the cross and receive the Gift from heaven that permeates this book.

I personally want to thank all the family and friends that have prayed for Kristen, stopped by for a visit, sent her encouraging notes or texts, or given her a call to brighten her day. We know this painful journey she is on requires a team effort, and there are so many faithful individuals who have supported Kristen for years. Your sustained persistence, coupled with our Heavenly Father's strength and grace, have been a major influence in Kristen's life. Thank you! Thank you! Thank you! May God bless you for your own personal sacrifice on Kristen's behalf.

To my daughter, Kristen. I am so proud of you! Taking on the challenge of writing and self-publishing a book seems ominous to me. You have always been a gifted writer. This attribute, coupled with your willingness to share your deepest feelings and be vulnerable with others, has resulted in a winning combination that will have a tremendous impact on all who read through these pages. You are and always will be my Little Princess. I am so thankful that I have had the privilege to be your father/King.

So, for those fortunate enough to have received a copy of this book, get a hot cup of coffee or hot chocolate, find a cozy chair and a warm blanket, and let this book pour life, encouragement and sunshine into your life.

Written by Cynthia Fox, my mommy.

Trust. Believing. Hoping. Words of life. The battle Kristen has encountered is extreme. The thoughts, actions and determination have either lifted her up or torn her down. These days, presently, she is living-NEVER GIVE UP! Why? She knows He dances over her. She knows without His compassion and kindness life would not be worth living. She has seen Him in many ways, but more recently in the 'little' things. The beauty of a sunrise or sunset. The ability to move, smell, and touch. The joy of seeing a bluebird or bunny during her day. The happiness that comes from knowing God and being known by Him. Restlessness comes and goes. Worry tries to control her, but fear of the 'what ifs' is slowly being left behind. She knows Whose hands are wrapped around her. Her life is His! She has walked many roads of discouragement but has chosen not to stay there. She is asking, seeking and knocking and she is finding rest for her soul in Him and Him alone. I'm proud of you Kristen and thank God for the example you are to me and many, many other lives. May you daily glorify Him-the King of Kings and Lord of Lords! Jesus, your everything!

Written by Kevin Fox, my little brother.

When I was first asked to write this for you, so many ideas ran through my head. I have so much to say! How could I write everything I want to say, without writing another book? Well Kristen, you are one heck of a woman. You have gone through mental battles that would wreck the strongest of minds. You have gone through pain, both physical and verbal, and yet you still push through. You have graduated from your dream college, even after spending a year in the hospital. You are still in pursuit of your dream of becoming a Physician Assistant. Kristen you have consistently gone to battle, and you have consistently won. The world has given you some scars, it has knocked you down, spit on you and it has continued to walk by; but hey, what's life without a few scars? What's life without a fight? I know that this life has been rough on you, and it isn't done yet. We are a family of rag tag foxes. We live messy, rough lives. We are always there for each other, and will do anything to take care of one another. We foster, nurture, and love anything or anyone that we come in contact with. Kristen, you have surpassed all of the expectations that were put in front of you. Everyone that is lucky enough to be in your life will leave with a full spirit of joy. Here's to the dreamers, so here's to you. Keep living with radiant joy and I will be with you. In front, to fight off your physical attackers, by your side, to fight off the spiritual, and behind you, supporting you when you feel as if there is nothing more for you in this life. I am proud to be your brother. Thank you for making my life worth living. -Kev

Preface

I started writing the essays, found within these pages and in the pages of my first book, *A Blessing in Disguise*, as a research project for school. It was my senior year of college. I volunteered for a lady who studied the lives of children living with cystic fibrosis. She gave these kids video cameras and asked them to record their lives. Then myself along with the other research assistants would transcribe the videos for her. During a team meeting, she asked us why we thought many kids didn't records the aspects of their lives that showed them receiving treatments or medication for cystic fibrosis. The majority said because the kids were embarrassed or shy. However, I spoke up and said I believed they tried to record their "normal people" activities because they didn't want their disease to define them. Instead, they wanted to show they could still live normal lives even though they suffered from a disease. Afterward, many research assistants shot down my theory and said that didn't make sense. I held my tongue because I feared if I said anything else I'd get too emotional.

The next time I worked on the videos I told the woman running the program that I could do more than transcribe videos. The main reason she studied these children was to research children living with a chronic disease. I expressed that I didn't have cystic fibrosis, but I did grow up with a chronic gastrointestinal (stomach) disease. If she desired, I could write essays about my own experience with a chronic disease. She agreed and I wrote my first essays for her on September 25, 2013.

From there I continued writing about different aspects of my disease and posted each essay on my CaringBridge site. For those who don't know about CaringBridge, I describe it as Facebook for sick people. On your site, you can post updates. People can visit your site to find out about your health battle versus calling, texting or e-mailing everyone with your latest health news. My surrogate grandma, Mel Kenaston, was the first to suggest that I put the essays into a book. I laughed and said that there was no way I could write a book. I majored in Health Science and minored in Spanish. I didn't have formal writing training and knew nothing about the publishing process. Furthermore, I didn't think any publisher would even take a second look at my work. However, Grandma Kenaston didn't give up and insisted that I try. She told me that I could send my essays to her husband's cousin, Janis Harris, publisher at Tyndale House Publishers. I finally agreed and sent the essays.

Two weeks later I had an e-mail from Mrs. Harris. She told me that an editor read my essays and said I could very well publish a book, but needed to write more before this became feasible. I received this response in February 2014. This news excited me, but I wanted to focus on graduating from college, before I thought about whether or not I would actually publish a book.

Months passed, I continued writing as ideas came and posted each essay to my CaringBridge site. I received feedback from various people who read the essays. Many asked me to put my essays into a published book. I still wasn't keen about a publishing venture, but realized God may have a different idea in His mind and He used other people to convey His plan to me.

After graduating from the University of Florida in May 2014, I explored the publishing world. The first decision I had to make was whether to find a literary agent to help me publish through a publishing company or embark on the self-publishing route. I chose the latter option.

As months passed, I prayed, sought counsel and received help from many different sources. I also continued writing during this entire time span. My writing started to diverge from what it's like to live with a chronic disease to topics I contemplated like how to find happiness or peace in sadness or the discouragement of depression. The first set of essays, which primarily were about my disease and family and friends were published in my first book, *A Blessing in Disguise*. I published that book on January 12, 2015. During the next few months I compiled the other half of the essays into this second book, *Blessings in Hidden Places*.

During this entire writing process, from September 25, 2013 to December 15, 2014, I realized writing has been therapeutic for me. I had feelings and emotions I didn't know I held on to that I have subsequently let go of during this process. I simultaneously began praying that God would allow me to trust His absolutely, perfect timing and stop basing my hopes on grades, school acceptances, test results, etc. By summer 2014, I could feel a change in myself. I recognized that health-wise, I was sicker than I had ever been in the past, yet more at peace with life than I'd ever been before. My parents and friends told me the anger they sensed simmering beneath the surface was no longer there and my eyes held peace they hadn't seen before. God was at work in my life— the writing I thought I did to benefit others, had actually changed me.

Introduction

It was merely a box of mac and cheese. It represented a quick and easy meal in the eyes of a college student or a busy mom, but an exciting treat for a little kid. However, for me, it symbolized hope. A reminder that someday I'd be able to eat this classic meal again because I'd win the battle I struggled to fight.

After completing my freshman year at the University of Florida, I came home (June 2011) excited to enjoy a Colorado summer with my family. I planned to work hard, so I could earn money for the upcoming school year and also take advantage of the neat opportunities Colorado presented. I worked as a CNA (certified nurse assistant), usually working six to seven days a week, six- to ten-hours-a-day. I competed in my first ten-mile and half marathon races. I climbed my first "14er" (a mountain peak exceeding 14,000 feet) with my daddy. I was at peak physical health. However, within a few months, my body changed so drastically that I could no longer complete any of these activities.

All my life I struggled with gastrointestinal (GI) complications. As a baby, I was labeled colicky. Time passed and Irritable Bowel Syndrome (IBS) was my diagnosis. The older I became, the harder it became to eat food. There was no rhyme, reason or pattern.

I have never been able to eat apples, tomatoes or things high in sugar. Digestion of these foods would cause a severe sensitivity where I would vomit for hours on end. When I entered high school, however, my food choices became more limited. Food high in fats and fibers would soon cause the same reaction. I would eat a salad and thirty minutes later I would vomit pieces of lettuce. It was difficult, but I learned to adjust. I thought I had reached the hardest point of my life; that I had climbed the mountain and could finally enjoy the view. Little did I know I had only climbed a foothill.

During the end of my first summer home from college, the pain I had when eating increased tenfold. I was forced to eat two meals a day but only in the evening. I would eat one meal around five or six o'clock in the evening and then another meal around ten or eleven o'clock at night. I only ate at night because the pain after eating was so severe that I couldn't function during the day. Nevertheless, most days I wasn't hungry when I needed to eat. I felt like I had eaten only a few hours beforehand. After eating I became so bloated that I looked like I was pregnant. Many times, I'd vomit food that I had eaten the previous night. This endless cycle continued for several weeks and I knew I needed to immediately contact my doctor.

The doctor ordered a gastric-emptying study (a study which measures how long it takes for food to empty out of your stomach) and the results came back severely abnormal. Because of these results, I had a G-J tube (gastro-jejunal tube-a tube which is surgically placed into your stomach and then threaded into your small intestine) placed inside me. I was released from the hospital a few days after its placement and told I should be fine to go home and eat and drink. However, when I tried to eat and drink, I began to vomit violently. I figured maybe my body was stressed and needed to adjust. Sadly, I was wrong. Over the next few days, whenever I tried to eat or drink anything I would vomit thirty minutes later. I had to be readmitted to the hospital for dehydration. This was when I realized I now climbed the mountain.

Throughout the next week, the doctors discovered I needed to have water added to my formula so I could stay hydrated while being fed. During the next few months, I readjusted to my new form of "eating" and "drinking."

Nevertheless, I continued to lose weight and reached a state of severe malnutrition. My 101lb. frame, at the beginning of the summer, had been reduced to an emaciated 78 lb. body. I was readmitted to the hospital because if I progressed further in the wrong direction my life would come to an abrupt halt.

So in January of 2012 I was re-admitted to the hospital until March of 2012. They changed my G-J tube to a G tube and slowly started to reintroduce food into my diet. I gained back all the weight I had lost and then some. I continued to see a nutritionist weekly until I had reached a weight of 115lbs. I was officially released from hospital care and began to run again. I was eating three meals a day, two snacks and received nightly feedings through my G-tube.

Everything was great, or so it seemed to all those around me. However, on the inside I was struggling. The doctors had told me that since I was now at a normal weight my digestion should improve and food would move through my digestive system without causing pain or discomfort. Their words couldn't have been further from the truth. The truth was that I felt like I was locked in a torture chamber. My stomach never felt empty. I was bloated all the time. I still suffered from immense pain every time I ate. I tried to tell my therapist what I was going through, but he merely told me not to focus on the pain and not to talk to anyone about what was going on. He said if I didn't acknowledge it or discuss it, then it would get better. It didn't get better... It only got worse.

I became moody and frustrated. I began to snap at everyone around me. Anger flickered behind my eyes. I tried to keep my feelings and thoughts contained and they began to eat away at me. I listened to my therapist and didn't tell my family what was going on. I felt trapped, alone and discouraged. I wondered how long I could keep up my façade and keep eating like I was supposed to.

I ended up going back to UF for half of the summer to catch up on some classes. The other half of the summer I was back in Colorado. I was happy to be running and working out again, but I was miserable. I still kept my feelings a secret and they continued to destroy me.

I went back to UF for my junior year of college in the fall of 2012. After the first month of being at school I realized I couldn't keep up my eating regiment anymore. It was making me too sick and I began vomiting after I ate. One day I called my mom and just started bawling on the phone. I told her everything that had been going on the last few months and how I felt like I was locked in a torture chamber, never able to get out. She asked why I hadn't told her sooner and I explained to her what my therapist had said. She told me that he was wrong to say that and that I shouldn't keep things like that from her or my dad. I learned that day what a serious mistake I had made by trying to keep my emotions and thoughts to myself. I vowed to learn from this mistake and not make the same error in the future.

During the time frame from June 2012-November 2012 I traveled back to Virginia three times to have a procedure done where they injected botox into my pyloric sphincter (the muscle sphincter between your stomach and small intestine). They were hoping that the botox would relax the muscle, hence allowing food to empty out of the stomach better. Sadly the procedure didn't yield any tangible results.

In late November of 2012 I traveled to Boston to go see a GI specialist at Boston Children's Hospital. I underwent some specialized motility testing and the results indicated that stomach emptying was slow. There wasn't much they could do except put me on a higher dose of medicine and send me on my way.

Over the next few years I continued to see doctors periodically and underwent a whole new round of testing. All the results came back indicating that there was slow motility of my digestive system, but everything that the doctors tried to fix it, wasn't working. During this time frame I successfully graduated from the University of Florida in May 2014. After graduation I came back home to Colorado.

During the fall of 2014 I submitted applications for PA (Physician Assistant) school and attended a few interviews. I chose to attend the University of St. Francis for PA school. The next session began in January 2015, but I requested to defer my start date until January 2016 for health concerns.

I was still locked in battle with my stomach disease. The 115lb girl from the summer of 2012 had once again reached a state of severe malnutrition and had lost 46lbs since that summer. It was January 2015 and I weighed a mere 69lbs. I knew that if I continued in this trajectory much longer, I would soon be dead. Hence, I requested that I start to receive my nutrition through my veins instead of my GI system. So on January 13, 2015 a PICC (peripherally inserted central catheter) was inserted into my right arm and I began to receive total parenteral nutrition (TPN) through the PICC line.

I began to gain weight once more since I no longer had to use my digestive system for food. The PICC line worked well for the first month, but then got displaced. When that happened they pulled out the PICC line in my right arm and put a new line in my left arm. The PICC line in my left arm never healed properly so eventually they switched my PICC line out for a central port, which was placed in my chest on April 10, 2015.

I continued on with life until I left for the Mayo clinic in Rochester, MN on May 25, 2015. When I first got to Mayo I thought I'd be there for a week max, much to my surprise I was there for almost a month. I went through a series of tests, which once again proved my stomach didn't empty. The condition known as gastroparesis. They decide to test out a TGJ (TransGastric Jejunal) tube for a second time. This tube went through my G tube but was then threaded down into the second part of my small intestine. They stitched the J part of the tube into my small intestine in order to prevent it from curling back into my stomach. However within a week the balloon holding the tube in place had popped, the stitches had ripped out and the J tube was back in my stomach. They decided to put in a permanent J (Jejunal) tube leading directly into my small intestine. I got my J tube on June 23, 2015. They ultimately decided to give me a J tube so that I could run drip feeds through my small intestine in order to keep it active so it wouldn't completely shut down. The drip feeds ran at 10-20cc's per hour which is the equivalent of 2-4 teaspoons an hour. Their ultimate hope is that I can continue to increase the rate as time progresses and not have to be dependent on the TPN for nutrition. While the TPN has been the only way I've been able to get adequate nutrition painlessly, it is causing my liver values to become elevated, which can eventually lead to a damaged liver.

So now we come to the present (July 2015), as I sit in my room, my fate is still undetermined. I'm still in a state of malnutrition and I can't eat or drink anything by mouth, but I'm still climbing my mountain because giving up has never been an option. My family and friends have stood by my side helping me every step of the way. People ask me how I cope and the honest answer is I can't cope alone. My Lord and Savior, Jesus Christ, is my strength, and those I love, encourage me on a daily basis.

Many ask what it's like to want to eat but to be unable to. I crave food, my mouth waters at enticing smells, and I have dreams about being able to eat. I want it so badly, but my body reacts to food like I consumed poison. The best way to put it is this: Imagine your favorite appetizer, entrée or dessert. Imagine how it smells, tastes and looks. Next imagine eating it. Savoring every single morsel. You feel fine after consuming it, but within fifteen minutes you start to feel weird. A tinge of nausea comes on, like maybe it wasn't cooked right or maybe a bad ingredient was mixed into the dish. A little later you have full-blown nausea. Your hands are sweaty and you feel jittery and shaky on the inside. Then it feels as though someone is punching you in the stomach while simultaneously trying to inflate your stomach like a balloon. The pain is excruciating and unbearable. All you want to do is curl up in a ball and wish it all away.

It doesn't stop there. Within thirty or forty-five minutes that delicious item you just ate is in your mouth again, just this time it's on its way out of your body instead of in. Funny though, at this point, all you want to do it is vomit. You want to purge yourself of whatever is making you feel like you're in hell. You want to be far from it. Soon the vomiting stops, but the pain doesn't. You still feel nauseous but nothing else will come up. You're weak and shaking from the stress your body endured.

Then stage two comes: You feel whatever food, which made it into your intestines, coursing its way through them, as if there is something alive inside of you. Moving throughout your abdomen. As it moves it appears to expand your intestines, pushing your abdomen out, causing you to look like you're pregnant. You pace back and forth, hoping that physical stimulation will move things through quicker. It may work and it may not, but anything is worth a try.

Finally, hours later you start to experience some relief. During that time, you'll vomit a few more times. Sadly, depending on the size of your treat you may continue to feel horrible for the next twelve hours. Sure, some relief will come in four to five hours, but total relief won't happen for twelve hours, when your stomach and intestines are fully empty. By twelve hours, though, you realize your body needs more fuel so that you can survive and the malicious cycle repeats itself.

That is how I've lived my life for the past few years. Every day I went through this vicious cycle until I got my PICC line. Soon after I got the line, the old cycle switched and a new cycle began where I vomited anything I ate or drank within the hour. Hence, it became pointless to eat since I retained zero calories and probably expended calories through vomiting.

I crave food every day. The body's need for food is so strong that you still desire that which causes you so much pain. Sometimes to stay sane I chew food and spit it back out to remember what it tastes like. I look forward to the day when I can eat once again and my food will actually stay down and move through my system pain-free. Whether that day will ever come is still to be determined. I can tell you this one thing though: I will not give up, no matter the pain or the agony. They say that in order to enjoy the view you may have to struggle up the mountain. Well, I'm determined to enjoy the view and one day soon that box of mac and cheese will transform itself into a comforting meal for me.

Heavenly Perspective

March 27, 2014

Panic. Uncertainty. Worry. Anxiety. I felt suffocated. It was as if each emotion weighed a thousand pounds and emitted a heavy cloud of smoke. This smoke enveloped me. I could sense it stretching into thin tendrils, each tendril encircling an air sac in my lungs. Not a single sac left untouched.

I make plans. Plans for the day. Study plans for exams. Plans to make plans. It keeps me organized. Centered. Confident. It gives me a sense of comfort and control. Go with the flow? You must be joking, I don't roll like that. At least for the majority of my life I didn't. "Going with the flow" was something I had to learn. It sure wasn't easy and I still haven't mastered it completely. I used to get so upset when my day didn't go according to *my* plan. When things didn't work out how

I'd planned them out, I'd get frustrated and lash out at others or panic and withdraw. I needed life to go according to *my* plan. Obviously, because it was the only sensible one.

My smart parents saw my obsession with planning and knew I'd never function in life if they didn't intervene. Why? They knew life throws more curveballs than straight ones. I, however, was resistant to their teaching. I didn't want to let go. I sure didn't want to let my day just flow. They persevered and slowly I saw wisdom in their words. Gradually, I learned to loosen up ever so slightly, but it was a long process. Nevertheless, it was worth it, because life threw me a curve ball no one could have imagined.

Fighting an illness was not part of my plan. Actually this illness reduced my life plan to a shadow of its former self. My life plan was a simple ten-step plan. Step 1: Graduate elementary school. Step

2: Graduate middle and high school. Step 3: Graduate College and Grad School. Step 4: Get a good job working in a hospital. Step 5: Get married. Step 6: Have kids. Step 7: See each of my kids off to college. Step 8: Retire. Step 9: Eventually see my children graduate, get great jobs and have a family of their own. Step 10: Die a peaceful death having lived a long and prosperous life with a wonderful husband and family. Well, I made it through the first step and a half, but after my freshman year of high school my plan went up in smoke.

During this time, my illness became more pronounced. Time passed and things appeared to get better, but I soon realized it was only a lull before the impending storm that broke the summer after my freshman year of college. This storm still rages, preventing my life from going according to any solid plan.

When that storm broke, I realized I was still far from the point of going with the flow. That first wave nearly drowned me. The weight of the panic, uncertainty, worry, and anxiety hindered my attempts to get my head above water. I began to fade because it became hard to combat the physical and emotional turmoil I was in. Then I heard it. Barely above a whisper.

Give it to Me, my child. If you allow Me to take your burden, then I can save you.

I almost missed the voice, for the storm was deafening, but then I heard it again.

My child let go. Trust Me! I can free you, but only if you let Me.

I knew I wasn't hallucinating. I had heard a voice. I responded, "Take it God because I can't handle it anymore." Then suddenly I could breathe again. The storm still raged all around me, but I could breathe! I no longer felt the weight of the emotions weighing me down. I then queried, "God, why are you whispering? I'd think You'd be a roar or sound like a storm ten times greater than this. Or even a lightning bolt. But a whisper? Isn't that anticlimactic? Furthermore, I've already accepted you into my heart, so didn't I already give it to you?"

My child I am your Father. I speak to you as My child. My whisper is enough. And yes you did accept Me into your life, but you never relinquished your desire to have complete control over your life. You gave me the position of assistant coach instead of head coach. I have tried to whisper to you numerous times to let it go, but you have brushed Me off. Or you have tried to convince yourself you gave control to Me. I see your heart and could see you really didn't give me control. However, you heard me this time because you had no strength to block me from convincing you to give Me control.

I hung my head in shame, realizing the mistake I had made. "I can't promise You I won't want control of my life again, but help me to choose to give You control, because I know I can't do it in my own strength."

My child, all I request is that you ask and I will give it to you. That you seek, and I will allow you to find what you are searching for. That you knock and believe that I will always open the door (Matthew 7:7, NIV).

Relief flooded me. "Then carry me Jesus, for I'll never survive this storm alone."

What you don't realize is that I've carried you for many years. You would have succumbed long ago if I hadn't been. You would have perished, but the day you accepted Me into your life, I vowed to carry you even before you gave Me complete control over your life. I knew you wouldn't make it without Me. Now that you are letting me take control you'll finally feel the arms that have surrounded you all along.

"Thank you Jesus! I know I'm so undeserving as my treatment of You has been subpar and not close to the treatment You deserve. Please continue to carry me through this storm, my Savior, because I don't know how long it will last or how much damage it will cause."

I thought you'd never ask. It is My joy to carry you, my child. Rest assured I do know when the storm will end. I do know how far you'll make it in this life. I know because I can see the big picture, a picture you'll never fully view.

"Did You cause this storm?"

I do not wish for my children to have to endure any storms. But life is undoubtedly full of them. I am

*here to make sure you survive
them, but I cannot fully assist you
until you ask Me to. You have three
choices, My child. You can choose
to accept My help and make the
best of this storm. You can choose
to accept My help and make the
worst of this storm. Or you can
choose to not accept My help and
succumb to the power of the
storm. The choice is yours. I
cannot force you to choose one or
the other.*

"I choose to make the best of this
storm, Jesus. I choose to accept
your help. Help me in achieving a
new goal. A goal to turn whatever
bad this illness causes me into
good for others. Let me be a
positive impact on others. Let me
touch their hearts and somehow
make their life a little better. Let
Your comfort, peace and love
surround them as I interact with
them. Let me never take another
day for granted. Help me, for I
know all of this is impossible on my
own."

I will, My child. You'll endure more pain and heartache than you can ever fathom. You'll have to fight on a minute-to-minute basis, but know I will be with you each step of the way. Even if you push me away, I will hold you. Only then, you won't benefit from feeling My arms around you. No matter what, I will never leave you. I will never forsake you. I will always be with you (Deuteronomy 31:6, NIV). That I promise.

I rested my head against His shoulder and slept peacefully, for my God had His strong arms wrapped around me and I knew I'd get through this storm somehow. I knew with God nothing was impossible (Matthew 19:26, NIV) and with His strength I could do anything (Philippians 4:13, NIV). I felt peace because He knew the plans He had for me. Plans full of prosperity and success (Jeremiah 29:11, NIV). So I gave Him control. As the years have passed, I've tried to take back control numerous times, and each time I do, I no longer feel His arms around me. He is a gracious and loving God. So each time I have realized my mistake He has extended grace and I once again feel those arms around me. I still plan my days. I still like to have control, but compared to the girl with her ten-step plan, I've changed. I don't have steps anymore, but each day I pray, "God, thank You for seeing the big picture when I can't. You know the perfect timing for everything. Let me be consumed by You and not by panic, uncertainty, worry, and anxiety." As a result, time and time again, I've been able to see just how perfect His timing is.

Worn

June 5, 2014

"I'm tired I'm worn/My heart is heavy/From the work it takes/To keep on breathing/I've made mistakes/I've let my hope fail/My soul feels crushed/By the weight of this world

And I know that You can give me rest/So I cry out with all that I have left

Let me see redemption win/Let me know the struggle ends/That you can mend a heart/That's frail and torn/I wanna know a song can rise/From the ashes of a broken life/And all that's dead inside can be reborn/Cause I'm worn

I know I need to lift my eyes up/But I'm too weak/Life just won't let up/And I Know that you give me rest/So I cry out with all that I have left" ("Worn," Tenth Avenue North)

This song came on the radio tonight and the words became my prayer. For I'm worn and, right now, the struggle seems incredibly hard. I cry out with all I have left for God to give me rest. Tears create rivulets down my cheeks because I'm exhausted from fighting. My heart broke as I sang along with the radio. I cry out with all that I have left for God to help me through this battle.

As the song continued playing I stood there and listened to the message. As I listened I contemplated several concepts. Many times people associate songs like this with health issues, coping with a loss or dealing with a struggle, but in reality this song can speak for anyone.

First, It pains me when people say, "Don't worry about how I'm doing or what's going on in my life. It's stupid stuff and nothing like what you deal with." I feel so sad when I hear people utter this. It's crucial everyone realizes the struggle in their life is not less important or less significant than the person next to them. Even if the other person's struggle is with cancer or losing a close family member or friend. Each person has his or her struggle to overcome and comparing your struggle to someone else's will only make it more difficult for you to deal with your own problems.

Are you worn right now? Are you struggling? Is your heart breaking over some matter? What are you hiding? Are you trying to be brave and "suck it up?" Let me tell you, true bravery is when you admit you hurt and you then let the healing begin. However, healing can't start and help won't come, if you try and manage your struggle on your own. Don't bury it because you think its "insignificant" or "not important." It is important, if it's bothering you, don't minimize it or your pain will increase. If you're reading this and you're struggling, if you're worn and tired, cry out to Jesus and talk to someone you trust (I'm here too.) because your problem is not insignificant and you can't manage it alone. Don't lie to yourself and try to convince yourself you can deal with it on your own.

Second, I have realized the perspective you have on life makes all the difference between how you live and how long you live on this earth. I wouldn't be on this earth anymore if I didn't have people who helped me keep a positive outlook on life. On days like this when the weight of everything seems heavier than ever, I realize I wouldn't still be here if I let those negative emotions, which leave me feeling worn, control my life. I'm still alive because I believe God fills my lungs with air because He isn't finished with me yet, here on earth. This perspective has kept me alive. The minute I adopt a negative perspective and I start wondering about my existence, I physically get worse. My pain intensifies, I'll feel more nauseous than ever, get dizzy, and my heart begins to beat faster. My symptoms will continue to get worse as my body starts to shut down. During these times, my will to fight isn't as strong. That's how I realized just how powerful perspective is and how it can determine the length of time you spend here on earth.

When you look at life with a positive perspective, life seems easier to handle. I've decided to stop letting my emotions get tied into every doctor's appointment. I refuse to let a bad report ruin my day. The reports I've had recently haven't been good, but I feel happier than I have in the past because I don't let bad news deter me from fighting. There is only one person who truly could give me bad news and that person is Jesus. When I get to the gates of heaven and I talk to my Savior, I don't want to hear how I failed Him because I let negative factors control me. Instead, I want to hear, "Well done my good and faithful servant" (Matthew 25:21, NIV). The only way I'll hear those words is by refusing to let things of this world stop me from pressing on in my fight. There is only one Person, who knows when I'll die. No matter what news I get, even if I'm told I only have so many days to live, I've decided I won't let it control me anymore. I admit I have to pray daily to keep that perspective because I can't keep up "face" like that in my own strength. However, once I made that decision, I started to see life in a different perspective. I still have days, like today, where I'm tired and worn, but I must keep pressing on. If I'm still breathing that means God still has a role for me to play on this earth and I want to win an Academy Award for that role.

So now, I ask you, What is your

perspective on life? It's perfectly human and normal to get sad, depressed, discouraged, disheartened by bad news. Yet, are you letting that bad news destroy you or are you choosing to take that bad news and make it as good as possible? Will you press on or will you give up? If you chose to not let bad news bring you down, you might be surprised how you don't feel down anymore. Sure, that bad news is still there, but can you change your perspective. If you're worn and you feel like life isn't worth it anymore or you wonder why you bother to try so hard, then cry out to the One who always listens. He will come; you may not feel it at the moment, but He'll be there for you. All He wants to do is comfort His hurting child. If you take Him as your Father, you'll be surprised how well He will fill that fatherly role.

Finally, listening to this song made me think about legacy. I may be worn, but another reason I don't want to give up is because I want to create my legacy for as long as possible. Your legacy starts when you're born, not after celebrating fifty or sixty years on earth. Your legacy begins the day you take your first breath and ends the day you no longer can breathe. If I give up while God still fills my lungs with air, I miss out on adding a new piece to my legacy. What will you be remembered for? You don't have to create a breathtaking masterpiece, sing a song that stays in the Top Ten for weeks, act in a movie that sweeps the Academy Awards or have five super bowl rings to have a great legacy. You may only be known in your own neighborhood, but you can still have a great legacy.

An amazing legacy is not just left by those who are famous. The greatest legacies are left by people who truly sought to do the best they could with the life they had. A great legacy is left by those who help others even though there isn't a newscast covering their good deed. Those who encourage the people around them. Those who work hard at their job, even though they may not receive any recognition. Those who smile at a stranger or hold the door open for the person behind them. You can leave a great legacy by trying to make the best out of your circumstances. You can leave a greater legacy than Hollywood's top star if you simply refuse to give up when life gets you down. Don't minimize the impact you may have on someone's life. Interestingly enough, some of the people with the greatest legacies became known only after they lived their lives. You don't know how much you may impact this world so start making your legacy now. Don't wait until you're "older" or "more grown up." The longer you wait, the more opportunities you miss making your legacy great.

Well, I sat down thirty-seven minutes ago to share the thoughts

I had as I listened to the song "Worn." I hope my rambling has inspired you and given you a new drive for your life. Remember, never give up, no matter how hard the struggle gets, because pushing on only makes you stronger. However, don't try to push on alone, for when you try to fight alone your chances at success are severely diminished. Be brave and ask others for help if you're struggling. For when you admit you're worn and need support, it's amazing how strong you'll feel afterward and how others' support can make your mountain turn into a molehill.

Let It Go

June 26, 2014

For those of you who haven't seen the Disney movie *Frozen*, I highly recommend you rent and watch it. It is a wonderful story and one I personally connected with. One of the most popular songs from the movie is "Let It Go". The song is great, but its title leads to an important lesson, one I'm finally starting to learn.

For years, I've been tied emotionally to the results and progress of my disease. I became hopeful each time I heard of a new possible solution or another test which might be able to shed more light on my case. However, time after time my hopes would be dashed as results came back with no definite conclusions. Newly invented solutions, which were extremely successful with other people, brought no relief to me. I was on an emotional roller coaster, placing my hopes and expectations on finding the "right" answer. Every time I heard a no, I'd close myself off. I'd become solemn when around others, and when I was alone, I'd use my pillow as a tear catcher.

About a year and a half ago, I finally realized I needed to "let it go." To not be emotionally attached to the progress of my disease. I needed to get off the roller coaster I kept riding because an accident was bound to occur. So, I let it go and gave it to Jesus. I decided I needed to change the way I looked at life.

I prayed, "God let me somehow grasp that Your timing is absolutely perfect. Nothing will happen that you don't already have control over. Help me trust that You will watch over me and direct my life just as it should play out." I've prayed that prayer for over a year now, and let me tell you—my life has changed.

I'm probably the sickest I've ever been. I know physically, I don't feel strong and vibrant as I'd like to be. However, I do feel more at peace than I've ever felt before. When I don't receive call-backs from potential places of employment or don't get accepted into a program I applied to or don't hear the answer I want from the doctors, I no longer feel a crushing, suffocating, debilitating disappointment. I'm sad or upset, but I'm not crushed. I get over it faster. I try to find a sliver of happiness in the moment of sadness. The funny thing is, when you're sincerely looking for it, you're bound to find it.

I feel lighter. Gray clouds reveal rainbows. Mourning turns to joy. Anxiety transforms to peace. The worries of the world don't seem so overwhelming. I feel like a smile adorns my lips more than it used to. I feel free. I still cry and become disappointed, angry or upset, but those feelings don't linger as long as they used to. If I go a few days without praying for that understanding, I'll start to feel myself trying to grasp for control again. That is when I need to remind myself to let it go.

Are there things in your life you're holding onto? Is there something you need to let go of? What's keeping you from feeling the peace I feel as I write this? Can you let go? Do you have the courage to release your safety blanket of misery? It's not easy and surely doesn't happen overnight. If you can do it, you'll feel an indescribable freedom and an uncontainable happiness. Dare to ask yourself what you need to let go. Face your fears. Be vulnerable and ask for help if you need it. You may grow more than you thought you could. You may see the world in a new light. The pain, the sadness, the hurt, the sorrow you're holding may weigh you down more than you realize. You may not fathom how much it crushes you and how close you are to suffocation. Let it go before you run out of air. If you're not sure you can do it, give it a trial run, so you can say you at least attempted the feat. Will you let it go or will you let it control you?

The Little Things

July 8, 2014

Are you so consumed with what happens in the future you forget to appreciate the present? Has your smile reached your eyes recently? Are you so focused on dreaming of what you want, that you unknowingly miss out on enjoying what you have now? Does your pursuit of happiness only bring frustration? How many people know the real you?

People have tried to discover the secret to happiness and contentment for years. There are countless books, movies, and resources to aid you in your search. Yet, even with these resources, ambitions, and directions, most people are not happy. Why? Who knows? It seems everyone has a different reason for the cause of their unhappiness. I've learned no matter what causes your inward storms, there is one consistent Person, who can make storms dissipate.

Jesus can calm any storm. I'm sure you've heard that numerous times and to be honest, you're probably tired of people shoving that down your throat. Perhaps you've given Jesus a chance and the storms still surround you. Perhaps you don't want to bother with that Jesus stuff because you see His story as fiction. Perhaps you have another random reason. I don't know, but before you stop reading, hear me out. Jesus *is* the answer to any storm. I know you probably think that's the religious answer. The book answer. The church answer. The answer that comes automatically, since I was raised in a Christian family. Well don't assume because I want to present you with a few questions. Do you think that answer brings me peace when I say it? Do you think I truly believe He's the only answer? Well, I'm gonna shock you because I'm

going to say no to those two
questions.

Yes, I cry out to Jesus during my
storms and also during calm times.
I cry out to Him because I don't
want to disappear during the
storm, and I know He is the only
one who can find me during the
storm and bring me to safety.
However, just believing Jesus is
there for me, or believing He holds
me, isn't the only thing I have to
do to find happiness in the storm.
Crying out to Jesus won't suddenly
make you happy. It won't bring
you contentment or joy. Saying the
words will do nothing. Believing
them will do something, but it
won't fix the entire problem. You
won't suddenly be better or happy
or satisfied with life. Jesus is the
first answer. However, He isn't the
final answer. What I mean is you
have to start living differently to
find the pure joy and happiness
you're seeking.

I've been mulling this concept over
for the past couple months. I have

Jesus, but I haven't always been happy or content with my life. I've been jealous of friends or people who have more money, cooler cars, take epic vacations or whatever. I've thought, *If only I had this or if only I could do that, I'd be much happier*. Well, that kind of thinking only caused me to become more despondent. Those thoughts caused my inward storm to rage stronger. I realized I needed do an 180-degree turn in my pursuit for happiness. Maybe I shouldn't even be on that pursuit because perhaps the act of pursuing happiness was actually making me sadder.

So I stopped pursuing happiness. I stopped trying to find a thing or person to make me happy. I began thanking God for what I had right now and for the new day He created, whether it was cloudy or sunny. I started appreciating little things in life. I looked for the happiness in my life versus dreaming of the happiness I could have. Guess what? When I started looking in the present, I started to worry less about the future and made amazing discoveries around me. I realized how I could find happiness sitting in the sun's warm glow, feeling its rays caress my cheeks and hair. I unearthed happiness in the music of the rain. I found it in the touch of the slight breeze or the push of a 20-mph wind gust. I discovered happiness while curled in my bed, surrounded by warm blankets. I uncovered happiness in my cup of tea with whipped cream. I located joy in my friends and families' warm embraces. I realized when I was thankful for the ability to walk, to drink, to smile, to see, that I felt happy on the inside. I was thankful for green grass, my adorable bird, a vehicle to drive, letters from people, clothes that weren't name brand, water to shower with and for safety and support. When I focused on these things, I had less time to focus on what I didn't have. A pure joy came that none could take away because I wasn't basing my joy on things hoped for, but things I had. I based my joy on moments I was living and not moments I was dreaming of. I found happiness in simplicity, which can lead to greater happiness when some of those dreams I have become a reality.

I started focusing on what I could do now versus what I used to be able to do. I found happiness when I stopped mourning what I lost because of my illness and focused on all I have gained or acquired and what I can still do. At one time, I cried over not being able to run anymore, but now I've stopped crying. I try to move on and appreciate what I can still do. I still become sad or bitter when I realize I'm missing out on something, but I have made an effort to move past the mourning and find the joy that exists in the sadness. While the past contains many timeless memories I will forever hold on to, I must not become consumed in wishing for things of the past, for then I'm not able to focus on the wonderful things that this present may contain.

Ever heard the phrase, "Don't judge a book by its cover"? Many times, I based my happiness or opinions on something or someone's "cover." Sometimes the worst "covers" contain the greatest treasures. How many times do we buy the name-brand, like Kraft® parmesan cheese, because we grew up using that brand and recognize the cover? Well, for two dollars less you can buy the Target® brand parmesan cheese, which contains the same cheese, but has a different or strange cover. I thought of this the other day while shopping and began wondering how many times I've lost "money" (a.k.a. happiness, friendships, etc.) because I based my opinions on someone or something's cover. I'm learning to stop judging by the "cover." I pray daily to not judge people. If God made them, then, in His sight, they are a masterpiece. I need to approach them with that in mind. Do I? Hardly ever, especially if their "cover" seems distasteful. I'm working on it though.

Also, how many times do we think we can have happiness if we have this brand of clothing, that type of car or real diamond earrings? Can we be happy when we have clothes that fit, a working car, and pretty jewelry? Can we look at those name brands, appreciate them, but also find joy in the things we have? I used to want the clothes from American Eagle®, Hollister®, Abercrombie®, Nike® or UnderArmour®. I thought if I had those brands I'd be happier. However, my happiness wasn't drastically altered when I had those clothes versus when I wore something from TJ Maxx®, Ross® or Goodwill®. I've found great clothes, which I wear all the time, from the latter stores. I'm pretty sure I didn't search for happiness within the name brands, I searched for acceptance and happiness I thought I'd receive from others because I wore the "cool" clothes.

This brings me to my last point. Do you base your happiness on others? I used to all the time. Sometimes, I still do. I wanted clothes from Abercrombie® and Hollister® when I was in high school because that's what the "cool" kids had. I wanted a convertible because I knew everyone would tell me I had a cool car. I wanted Tiffany and Company® jewelry because that is what the other girls wore. I thought if I had these things I'd be accepted or make more friends. (Just as a side blurb—sometimes I do buy things from Nike® or American Eagle® because I like the item because it's comfortable, fits well or brings me joy, but I'm not buying it in order to be accepted. Nevertheless, the majority of the time, in the past, I would lean toward "branded" items because they were name-brands and I thought popularity would follow me if I purchased them.)

If you're making your choices in life based on how you think others will treat you, you'll ultimately be more upset. The reason for this is because you're buying things in hopes of being accepted instead of making the purchase based on whether it's something you really like or not. I haven't learned how to overcome this, but I'm trying. I try to make choices based on what I want, not what I think others will like. When I do make decisions based on what I really want, I'm happy. I'm happy because I start out with happiness. When I make a decision based on what I think someone else will want, I may never end up happy. Interestingly enough, many times I don't get the reaction I hoped for from others.

I'm learning, I'm growing, and I'm trying new things. As this process continues, I'm beginning to find happiness in more and more places. This is a journey I want to continue because I'm learning things I didn't think I could. Nevertheless, I won't be completely happy until I am in heaven. So while I'm here on earth, I'll focus on what I can tweak in my life in order to allow more happiness to enter. Will anyone join me on this journey? You might be surprised how much happiness you find when you stop your "pursuit of happiness" and focus on the joy that already surrounds you.

Beat Again

July 12, 2014

My mom told me the story behind Phillips, Craig & Dean's song, "Tell Your Heart to Beat Again." This is the story: A surgeon performed open-heart surgery on a patient and everything went well. He had already put in the new heart and massaged it so that it would start beating again. However, the heart refused to beat. The surgeon tried everything he could to get the heart to start, but to no avail. Before he deemed the surgery a failure, he removed his surgical mask, bent down and whispered in his patient's ear, "The operation went perfectly, your heart has been repaired. Now, tell your heart to beat again." After he had said this, the patient's heart began to beat again.

This surgeon could only do so much. However, the greatest Surgeon of all, God, can make major repairs in your life, if you let Him. Medicine has seen this phenomenon time and time again. The patients who are predicted to die, but who desire to live—live. Those who are predicted to survive, but have no will to live—die. It is a phenomenon that many know about, but few choose to address. Why? We don't want to face the truth that we need to do more than rely on medicine, doctors, teachers, parents or whatever to find healing or success. We first and foremost need the drive inside of us to live.

Many times people say they want to pull through, they want to do better, they want to succeed, but deep down they know the truth. They know they've already given up. They may hold on a little longer, but ultimately they don't last because their will is gone. Before you get upset, let me say one thing: Just because someone died, doesn't mean they gave up. I know plenty of people who fought hard for their life and lost that fight. Sometimes we fight with every breath in our body and God decides He wants us home, and once God has decided that, no amount of fighting will prevent that from happening. Nevertheless, there are many people who appear to be fighting and say they have the will to live, but deep down they've given up. You can act like you want to get better or that you'll never give up, but on the inside you've succumbed to whatever battle you face. No one may ever find out you've given up. People may still believe you have the will to continue on. Ultimately though, it doesn't matter what other people know because your lie is only hurting you and bringing you closer to your end.

It may seem like this just applies to medical conditions, but it doesn't. It can apply to any area of your life. If you don't have the will or drive to succeed, you most likely won't. It doesn't matter how many times you tell others you want to succeed or you're trying. If you really aren't trying, then you won't find success. It's as simple as that. As you hurt yourself with your lie, you may also start to hurt those around you through your attitude. Your lie may also begin to affect how you're performing in school, the way in which you work or various other aspects of your life. No one may ever find out you lied, but they may start to experience the repercussions of your lie.

The placebo effect demonstrates the power of every person's will. For many years, I've heard of study after study that has shown the group given the placebo (usually a pill made of sugar) experienced greater results and reported more progress than groups given the real drug or nothing at all. Scientists concluded the only way these results occurred was because the people given the placebo were convinced they were taking a new, amazing drug that would bring them relief from whatever plagued them. They believed the placebo would fix the problem, so it did. The mind is so powerful. It begs to question whether you use your mind to its full potential and whether you use it to fuel your will or deplete your will. Even if you convince others that you're trying, but in your mind you aren't, then you won't achieve the results you could have.

I have seen this play out in my own life. Doctors, friends, family, and strangers will see me and ask me if I'm better or tell me I look good, maybe a bit skinny, but I look good. Then the doctor will look at my blood work and my vitals and they'll see how poor my health really is. They become surprised I'm still walking around and functioning normally. What causes this juxtaposition? I have a will to live. That will isn't always as strong as I'd like it to be, but it's still there. It's this drive to live that has kept me alive.

It is a will fueled by the love I've received from so many. The moment I lose my will to live, I will die. At that point, my body couldn't sustain itself because it would not be fueled by my drive to live. I tell myself daily that today can't be my last day. I tell my GI system to begin to move again. I tell myself don't ever give up. Plus I pray those things too. That is why I'm still here today. Sure, God may decide my time has come and no amount of will can stop His call home, but until I get that call, I must continue to live.

This doesn't mean that if I never get better, I didn't try hard enough. The surgeon had to massage the heart and perform the operation in order for the patient to be able to tell their heart to beat again. Therefore, a person's drive to live or succeed isn't the only thing allowing them to live or be successful. Outside help is also necessary for healing. However, if a person doesn't have that drive then their chance of survival or success decreases significantly.

People all over this world blindly go through their daily routines, convincing others they are fine, when on the inside they have lost their will. So many people are crying, breaking and hurting on the inside. Are you one of those people? Have you given up on something? Have you lost your will to fight for whatever is in front of you? Have you convinced others you're fine and you're trying? Are you burying that pain, guilt or sadness far below your exterior so no one can see the lie you tell them? Is there a part of your life you need to tell to beat again? Have you told so many lies you've begun to believe them yourself? Are you giving in to your lies and in turn hurting yourself even more?

When you've lost your will, you automatically begin a downhill descent toward disaster. It may be a slow descent taking years to crash or it may be a fast one, crashing within a week. However, if you're not dead yet, then you can still find your will again and heal from that crash. If you haven't crashed yet, you can divert your path away from disaster. It won't be easy, especially not at first. It will take more energy, strength, and resolve than you thought you needed, but you can do it. You can find your will again and divert your path and/or heal from the crash you just had. You may not see the results right away, and you may still want to give up, but you have to decide not to. Remember, even if you try to lie about it you're only going to hurt yourself the most so do yourself a favor and throw all those lies away.

You also can't do this alone. My will is fueled by my faith and the love and support I've received and continue to receive from others. God is always able and ready to add fuel to your empty tank. He adds it to mine every day. Actually, it's probably the main reason I can get out of bed in the morning because I beg God for the strength to get up. Once you've decided to fight whatever you're up against, find someone you trust and respect, and open up to him or her. You may be surprised how much easier it can be to carry your burdens when you no longer feel like you're carrying them alone. As you open up, you will start to feel that fuel being added to your very empty tank. You may also be surprised to find your heart beginning to beat again.

Pluck For Pain

July 25, 2014

Sometimes you put yourself through pain in order to hide the deeper pain. You can't understand this unless you've done it. You try to understand. You try to sympathize, but you don't know what it's like unless you go through it. Pretending to understand what someone else is going through doesn't make it any better for them, so it's best to acknowledge you don't comprehend it. Instead, just be there for the person.

I know what it's like to put yourself through pain in order to disguise a deeper pain. I've used this technique to distract myself from my GI pain. In order to draw my mind away from the intense pain caused by my digestive disease, I will pluck my underarms versus shave them. I'm sure about ninety-nine percent of you are either cringing or think I'm weird. Think whatever you want, but you know what? It works! It actually isn't painful for me to pluck my underarms. I barely feel it because my other pain is so much worse. Nevertheless my technique to block my deeper pain, is safe and doesn't cause me bodily harm. Many other people also put themselves through pain in order to hide their deeper pain.

It's extremely difficult to understand why someone struggles with cutting, commits suicide or lashes out at others. We can't perceive the pain they go through. It's hard to fathom someone would choose to inflict pain on themselves. However, what many fail to realize is that the person can't even feel the pain they inflict on themselves because the other pain they are feeling is so much worse.

Most people react in the worst way possible when they hear someone physically harmed themselves. They get upset or angry with the person, even telling them they were stupid to do that. When they attack the person, it only adds fuel to the deeper pain. This causes the person to inflict more pain on themselves. It becomes a cycle. A dangerous one. Often a secret one. Unfortunately, also a deadly cycle that takes many lives.

What can you do? Well, it depends what side you're on.

If you're a person trying to bury the deeper pain, you need to know you aren't alone. You need to know everyone isn't against you. Everyone doesn't hate you. When you feel surrounded by pain and darkness, there is still hope and light.

You need courage to find the hope. You must be brave and call out for help before your voice is gone. You must make an effort because if you don't you'll fall farther than you imagined. Even when death seems like the best option, it really isn't.

I know you've heard that a thousand times, but will you be courageous and believe it? Are you willing to experience a little more pain so healing can occur? Are you willing to step out on a limb to save yourself? All you need to say are three words, Help me Jesus. He will come.

You may not feel it at first. It has taken me almost a year of praying *daily* to feel a peace and happiness I haven't felt before. Yes, I'm in pain. I'm suffering from a deep, daily, hellish pain, but I've found peace. I've found happiness. I'm content. Yet, it took a year or more to get to this place. A year of crying out to God for help. A year for God to show me how to trade anger and frustration for happiness and peace. So how can I turn the simmering rage into a sparkling smile? How can I convert the deep anguish into a genuine joy? Let me tell you.

Your rough road won't become smooth overnight, and that is

probably the scariest part. You'll experience pain before true healing occurs. The healing will come, but it will hurt like none other. You must push through it in order to experience life-changing healing. Don't give up or you'll miss out on things you could never fathom, and you won't be able to make the impact you could have. Reach out to Jesus and those you love and trust so you won't be alone in your battle. The hardest thing to do is admit you're hurting. If you do this, then the healing will occur much faster.

If you're on the other end of the spectrum and you don't understand why someone would inflict pain on his or herself, then stop trying to understand it. You will probably never understand someone else's pain. It's impossible because every single person in this world is unique and no one goes through the same experience in the same way. No one can understand someone else's pain. We try. We try mighty hard, but trying can leave us frustrated and annoyed. It can make us so reactive that sometimes we end up hurting that person more and making the situation worse.

I understand what it's like to mask a deeper pain with different pain. Even though I get this, I'm foolish to pretend I understand someone else's pain. So I stopped trying to understand and instead try to love and listen to them.

If I'm venting about a problem sometimes, I just need to vent. I don't need someone to solve the problems for me; I need them to listen. Hence I try to do the same for others. I'll give suggestions if asked or if it's appropriate, but I try not to make them feel as if I'm solving their problems. I want them to feel like someone is there, listening and caring for them.

I also love them. It doesn't matter what they've done, how they may have injured themselves or what is in their past. People who are hurting *need* love. Love can be more effective than the therapy and medicine they receive from the medical field. Loving someone can save a life, change a viewpoint, and in turn impact the world.

No matter what side you're on you have to be brave. It takes courage to face the pain and it takes courage to show love to the hurting. In either case, you'll have to depart from your comfort zone, but once you leave it, you'll look back and wish you'd left sooner.

Beating Around the Bush

August 2, 2014

Who are you living for? That's the real question. Many of us say we live our lives for ourselves, but is that truth? Have we lied to ourselves so much we now believe the lie is the truth? Let's be honest here. I am almost one-hundred percent sure we think we live for ourselves, but, in reality, most of us live our lives for others.

Let's make this distinction. You may live your life to help others, look out for others or serve others. Those are all good things. However, what I'm referring to is when we try to live our lives how we think others want us to. We tiptoe around issues because we don't want to offend someone. We wear certain outfits because everyone else does. Half the time we don't even choose a movie because we really want to watch it, we choose a movie because we think it's what everyone else wants to see. We pick a restaurant because we think it's where everyone will enjoy eating. Why do we do this?

The root of it is fear. We're afraid to make a wrong choice or make a choice that appears wrong in others' eyes. We're afraid we'll be ridiculed because we don't have the newest fashions or the fanciest car. We're scared others will ostracize us. We let fear control our feelings, and in doing that we fail.

Does this resonate with anyone? It does with me. I've acted in this manner and continue to act this way. Nevertheless, I'm trying to change and thus overcome the fear I have of failing in the eyes of others. I want to stop tiptoeing around issues I think will offend my friends. If they are my true friends, they'll accept me for *my* beliefs, *my* opinions, and *my* actions and love me no matter what. If they can't or won't, then they most likely aren't a true friend. If they aren't a true friend, then they are probably a "comfort zone" friend. A "comfort zone" friend is one who leaves when life or relationships get tough.

I've had plenty of experience with these types of people. I ended up hurting myself by trying to appease them. I tried to say and do things around them I thought would keep them happy. It worked. They were happy, but that is not a foundation for a true friendship. When life got real, and I became sicker, I couldn't convince them everything was fine and dandy because my body betrayed my words. The situation was tough for them and they disappeared from my life. At first, it caused me heartache. Ultimately, though, it was for the best because I'm trying to commit to being as real and transparent as I can. This way I know the foundations of my relationships will hold true.

I'm not saying you have to be transparent with everyone. Some things really aren't anyone's business except your own. Some things are better kept to yourself. If you utilize your God-given wisdom, then it will be easy to determine what to say, who to say it to, and when to say it.

The point I'm trying to make is sometimes we make decisions, which leave us unhappy and frustrated in order to please someone else. Other times we "change" our viewpoints so people won't judge us for the opinions we have. Is it scary for me to admit I follow Jesus? Sure! I brace myself for retaliation. Sometimes I don't even bring it up because I'm scared people's opinions about me will change. I don't like to talk politics because I don't want to debate about various issues in our world. Insecurity fuels my silence. Fear blankets my insecurity and the combination of the two causes me to act in ways I shouldn't. Fear and insecurity cause me to buy certain clothes, choose movies I wasn't interested in, go places I think are boring or lie to others about my opinions or views.

One more point, sometimes in a relationship, you do things you aren't fascinated with, go places that bore you or watch movies which don't hold your interest because you care about the person you are with and want to do things they enjoy verse always doing what you want to do. However, if you pretend those are also your favorite things you're lying. Be honest and say you don't like that movie, but if they like it, you'd love to see it with them because you care about them.

Being honest will kill the relationships which aren't meant to last, but will strengthen the relationships that are there for the long-term. We all need to grasp that and apply it to our lives. We'll only make ourselves miserable trying to please everyone at all times. We'll end up hurting ourselves over and over until one day we just explode. I don't feel like exploding sometime in the future, so I've decided to stop tiptoeing around topics with my friends. I will respect their opinions, listen to what they have to say, and hope they return the same favor. Trust me, they will, if they are true friends. I want to stop going to the store and buying things I think will help me gain others' approval. I want to do or buy things because that's what I want to do and not because I think that is how everyone else wants me to be. I want to stop saying and doing things, which make other people happy, but leave me upset and frustrated. I want to stop living a lie and start living the truth.

I've started applying these principles and so far I've only gained happiness and peace. Therefore, I'd call it a successful experiment, which needs to turn into a life application. Will you take the risk too and begin this experiment in your life? If you do, I earnestly hope your results are as positive as mine have been.

ASK

August 5, 2014

We seem to forget Jesus's ASK promise. "Ask and it will be given to you; Seek and you will find; Knock and the door will be opened to you" (Matthew 7:7).

Ask and it will be given to you. We read this and doubt its validity because we have asked for things and haven't received what we asked for. However, is that just an assumption we are making? Because, in reality, each time I have asked it has been given to me. If you put aside your pride, selfishness, bitterness, etc. you will see what I have discovered. The funny thing is it hasn't always been given to me in the way I asked. I have asked God numerous times to heal me. I used to think He answered with a no, but I can now see He has healed me. He has healed my heart, which I didn't realize was hurt and broken. My

heart healed through
the experiences I've had because
of my disease. God surely did
reply, just not in the way I'd
prayed for. Instead, He saw what
really required healing in my life.
He saw what I couldn't and in
doing so answered my prayer in
the way I truly needed it answered.
He always answers, it just may not
be the answer we hoped for or
expected. We don't always see it
like that because we don't realize
what we're asking for could
actually hurt us more. God will
always answer us in ways that
protect, comfort and benefit His
precious children.

Seek and you will find. We have to
consider if we're seeking the right
things. The promise holds true for
anything we seek after. If we seek
after the wrong things in life, we'll
find trouble. If we seek after the
right things in life, we'll find
peace. We must carefully evaluate
what we seek. If we say one thing,
but our heart tells a different story,

we won't find what we say we're
looking for.

Now what about miracles? Jesus
performed them, the disciples did
them, countless witnessed them,
but now-a-days many of us believe
miracles are a thing of the past.
Sure we hear about the person
who miraculously gets better, or
about that collision that almost
happened or the extra twenty
dollars that someone found to pay
the bills. Yet, we also
question: How come the seas don't
part for me like they did for Moses?
Why won't my child rise from the
dead? How come loaves of bread
and small fish aren't multiplying for
my hungry family?

Instead what we should be asking
is for God to give eyes to see the
miracles permeating our world.
Miracles we miss out on because
we're looking for them in the
wrong places. We want those
declared dead to be alive again,
like the people raised from the
dead in the Bible. We wonder why

our disease sticks around and doesn't disappear as the leper's sores did. We contemplate why the storm, we are praying to abate, continues to rage. As we question, we become blind and resistant. We stop looking for miracles and instead decide miracles were just things of the past.

I thought miracles were a thing of the past. Through this assumption, I made myself blind to the ones swirling around me. What I needed to do was start with the basics and work up. Now, I see a miracle in the way my bird responds to my voice. I consider it a miracle that I was placed in a family who supports and loves me more than I deserve. I see a miracle in my illness because otherwise I wouldn't have a passion to help those who are also hurting. I also wouldn't be able to adequately relate to suffering. I wouldn't be able to reach out to the people I've been able to. I see a miracle in how God worked in my life these past years. I see a miracle in God's perfect timing for everything. I see the miracles because I'm truly seeking them. God promised me if I sought, I'd find. If you seek, you too will find, for God has never broken a promise.

Knock and the door will be opened to you. Are we knocking or pretending to knock? That is the real question. We may convince those surrounding us we have this amazing relationship with Jesus and the door is wide open. However, we can't lie to Jesus. If we pretend to knock, it won't fake Him out. You have to really knock in order for the door to open. Yet, we hesitate because we're afraid of what life lies behind the door. We're afraid to give up our wants and desires and to let Jesus in. Too many people assume once they let Jesus into their life, it will consist of Bibles, praying, pastors, uncomfortable Sunday clothes, G-rated movies, and every other innocent thing associated with the image of the church. Well, let me tell you, that image is *way off.* Once you follow Jesus you don't become the judgmental, rigid, fake people that everyone seems to picture when they hear the title "Christian." I do lots of fun things in my life and go on exciting adventures. I go to parties and watch R-rated movies. Yet, I've also been a follower of Jesus through it all.

Now let's say we've knocked and we aren't pretending, but we feel like the door remains shut in our face. What we forget to check is if we opened our door to Jesus. Are we just asking Him to open His door for us, but not opening our door to Him? If we don't open that door, how is He supposed to get in? I'm sure you're thinking, *Well can't Jesus walk through walls?* The answer is yes, but He can't walk through the walls you build because He will never force Himself on anyone. I encourage you to

make sure you've opened your
door for Him. Once you open your
door, you may be shocked to find
the door you've been knocking on
opened long ago when you first
knocked.

When we forget Jesus's ASK
promise, we tend to live a more
miserable life. Take a second and
evaluate your own life. How has
this promise come true and how
does it continue to prove true.
After you take a moment to
evaluate this you may discover
countless things you've missed and
your outlook on your life could
change.

A Punishment?

August 21, 2014

This essay is dedicated to Kellyn Rolfe who shared this verse one day, with me, in order to encourage me.

"As he passed by, he saw a man blind from birth. And his disciples asked him, 'Rabbi, who sinned, this man or his parents, that he was born blind?' Jesus answered, 'It was not that this man sinned, or his parents, but that the work of God might be displayed in him.' "(John 9:1-3, NIV).

Multiple times, I've had people tell me maybe my parents or I need to repent from a sin and then perhaps I'll be healed. I try to calmly thank them and ask they never again blame my parents for my disease. Blaming me is fine, but when you try and blame my parents, that's crossing the line. My parents have suffered more than I, through this disease, and it's not their fault I have this illness. In all honesty, it's not anyone's fault. Perhaps I have this disease so "the work of God might be displayed in" me.

How many times do we wonder if the bad things happening to us are really a punishment from God? How many times have we asked Him why? How often do we make the bad things worse because we lament their presence in our lives? What if we started treating the bad things as challenges and gifts from God, so His work and message might be displayed through our response? Do you think your life would change dramatically? Do you think your suffering would diminish?

I would respond with a vehement "yes" to the previous two queries. I know I've increased my suffering when I respond negatively to the bad things crossing my path. When I accept the disappointment, despair or agony, while simultaneously trusting God has a plan, I don't suffer as long. I feel peace and happiness sooner. Plus, the burdens of disappointment, despair, and agony seem to become significantly lighter.

Obviously, our instinctive response to any bad thing coming our way is disappointment, anger, and sadness. Yet, if we suppress that instinct we may find blessings disguised in the "punishment." However, if we don't look for those blessings, they'll remain hidden and we'll only wallow deeper in our negative emotions. If we treated every "punishment" or hard time in our life as a hidden treasure, we may begin to respond to these bad times with joy instead of anger, happiness instead of sadness, and excitement instead of disappointment. If we treated every disease, negative emotion, heartache, as a gift, then we would be able to improve our lives and, simultaneously the lives of those around us.

If we treat our hardships as punishment, we'll act like someone who has been harshly reprimanded. We'll sulk, become depressed, lack joy, and we'll be miserable. As we act in this manner, we'll also negatively affect those around us because one person's bad mood is extremely contagious to anyone they interact with. That person's anger, depression, disappointment will radiate from them. Anyone who comes into contact with that person will feel the ramifications of those emotions. We not only cause ourselves to suffer more, but we inadvertently cause all who come into contact with us to suffer. Negative emotions are highly contagious so you'll infect all who are around you with those same emotions.

On the other hand, positive emotions are also extremely contagious. Therefore, responding positively to the negative circumstances in your life will infect others around you with the same joy, happiness, and peace you radiate. You'll bless others through your suffering and touch people's lives.

No, it's not easy to respond positively to the negative circumstances. Yes, it takes great strength to fight off the depression, despair, anger, and sadness, and transform those emotions into joy, peace, happiness, and fulfillment. Yet, once you do, your world around you radically changes. You begin to look at it with a new set of eyes, filled with wonder.

You'll see how your pain brings healing to others. How through your sadness you can bring happiness to someone else. Your depression will allow you to help others find joy. You can morph your despair into hope for others. As you see this happen, you'll uncover treasures hidden in your "punishment".

If you accept your bad times as a way for the works of God to be displayed through you, you'll feel a new purpose for your life. Your "punishment" won't seem like a burden. I guarantee you'll begin to feel peace and happiness you never thought you'd feel. You'll begin to see a change in others too. You'll realize the impact you can make in other people's lives as you go through your hardships.

I have begun to thank God for my disease. I know this sounds strange, but I've found when I approached my disease in this light, I see all the good coming through my trials. I don't think I would be as empathetic towards those suffering if I hadn't suffered first. There are countless people I wouldn't reach if I hadn't first experienced the deep pain that is associated with fighting against seemingly insurmountable odds.

Growing up going to hospitals ignited in me a passion for working in a hospital one day. When my future patients come to see me, I can truthfully tell them I know what it's like to be in terrible pain, to feel hopeless, to want to give up on life and to be sick on a daily basis. I can encourage them not give up by explaining to them if I have given up, I wouldn't be here talking to and helping them. I can form connections with people others may not be able to because of the things I've experienced through my disease.

I'm 100 percent sure I wouldn't have been able to help the people I have helped if I didn't have my illness. Coming to that realization has made all my struggles so worthwhile. If I were able to go back in time and choose whether or not I had to live my life with this disease, I believe I'd choose to live life with it. Why? I've helped people through their own trials. I've pulled some back from "a cliff" that they were ready to jump off of. I don't like being sick or in pain, but if this is the only way I save others, then I'll bear my burden gladly. I ask God daily to allow my suffering to bring healing to others. By God's grace, I've seen that prayer answered. Furthermore, I know there are probably other examples of people I have been able to touch, which I won't find out about until I get to heaven. You never truly know how many you touch on this earth until you get to heaven. Don't think your suffering hasn't been worthwhile.

If you let yourself be used by God, He *will* use you and your life will dramatically improve. Your hardships will be much easier to handle. Your sadness and depression will seem insignificant because your happiness and joy will increase dramatically. The only thing you'll wonder is why you didn't start acting like this sooner.

Soul

August 26, 2014

I have heard it said before that "They can cut your body, but they can never cut your soul." Whether or not you've heard this saying isn't important, but the message contained within it is critical. Because, in reality, how many of us actually believe or portray this message?

I believe the saying is 100 percent true. Your soul is yours and yours alone, but these days it seems like we've forgotten that very important fact. We're the only ones who can "cut" our soul, and too often that's exactly what we do, yet we blame it on external sources.

What exactly is a cut? Well, it's basically any negative thing in your life. It doesn't refer to a physical cut like during an operation. A cut is something that hurts us deeply and has a profound negative impact on our lives. It could be a divorce, a broken engagement, a gut-wrenching diagnosis, a denial from a dream school, a bad grade, depression, anxiety, anger, sadness, bitterness, abandonment, rejection, or even abuse. The cut could be deep or shallow, regardless though, it still hurts and leaves a scar even after it's healed. A scar, which sometimes doesn't heal properly and leaves a red, ugly, distorted mark on us.

The cut always begins with an outside source. However, when the cut reaches our soul, the source is internal. We're the only ones who can cut our soul. We cut our souls by succumbing and becoming overwhelmed by the external cut. We never cut our soul at first, but as we hold onto the negative event or emotion and refuse to let it go, we damage our soul. We slowly carve away at it and become deeply imbedded in that negative event or emotion.

When we cut our soul, our pain becomes amplified and all who are around us see our wounds. We may try to keep them hidden, but as we cut deeper, our disguises begin to fade and our pain begins to show through. We see the pain in others manifest itself as drug overdoses, suicide, anger, depression or even erratic behavior.

Take comfort that you have the power to stop your soul from being damaged, since you're the one who cuts it in the first place. That power only grows when you ask the Omnipotent God to supply you with His strength. He will help you; you only need to ask. Furthermore, as the Great Physician, He can simultaneously heal the wounds you've inflicted on your soul. Wounds that tear you apart.

The question remaining is; how do we stop ourselves from cutting our souls? The answer is simpler than you'd think. You must not let the negative things injuring your exterior, breach into your interior. You must not internalize the negative, for once you've internalized it, you've essentially sharpened your proverbial knife and started to slice away at your very soul. Unfortunately, it's easier to tell yourself not to internalize the negative than to actually do it, especially, when you're drowning in the negative emotions and events that rage around you.

Trust me, I know from experience. I battle every day to keep my knife dull and my soul whole. Let me tell you, it's an epic battle leaving me drained and worn. Thankfully, Jesus is there, literally pouring His strength into me, giving me the ability to keep fighting. Over a year ago, I decided that the University of New Mexico was my top choice for PA schools. As I prepared to apply there this year, I realized the deadline for the application was

August 1, not September 1, like I'd
first thought. Sadly, I realized this
on August 10. The damage was
already done. I wouldn't be
applying to the school I'd chosen
as my first pick. I came to a
crossroads. I could either let the
negative external event cause me
to cut myself internally or I could
have faith that God's plan was
perfect and it'd work out in the
end. I chose the latter option and
in doing so I avoided damaging my
soul. I also avoided the pain,
regret, and overwhelming sadness
I had felt at other times when I
chose the former option. However,
this time, since I chose the latter
option, I felt strangely at peace
and life went on. If I had chosen to
cut my soul, I assure you I'd still
hurt now.

Remember the popular phrase
"make lemons into lemonade"? It
has a ring of truth to it. Lemons
are the negative things in your life.
You can take those negative
things, internalize them and cut

your soul or you can get busy making lemonade and distract yourself from inflicting wounds on your soul. It's not an easy task, by any means. It's much simpler to cut your soul. However, when you do, you miss out on the opportunity to enjoy a fresh cup of lemonade. Making lemonade takes effort just like it takes a great amount of strength to stop yourself from damaging your soul.

If you feel overwhelmed by the lemons in your life, think how much lemonade you'll be able to make. You'll have enough lemonade for yourself and some left over to share with others. When you share, you may prevent others from making a cut on their souls. When they get a taste of your lemonade, they may be motivated to turn their own lemons into lemonade as well.

Internalizing the external negative things will only cause you more pain. It will not bring you joy or satisfaction. Sure, it's an easy thing to do, but the damage left behind is extremely difficult to repair. Like other things in life, taking the easy road usually causes more difficulties in the long run than if we'd initially started out taking the challenging route. Fortunately, the challenging route gets easier as you walk farther down the path. You'll still have to fight, but the victory will be sweet and your soul will remain whole.

Choose today what you'll do. Start now and stop letting those external negative events morph into internal cuts on your soul. Make yourself some lemonade. Use it to refresh yourself as you walk down your life path. Share some of that lemonade with those around you and watch as they put down their knives and healing happens in their souls too.

Judged

August 31, 2014

So far in my life, I've not met a single person who likes to be judged. Yet every person I've met has judged another. What creates this hypocrisy? We all know the Golden Rule, "Treat others as you want to be treated," yet we seldom apply it to our lives. Why? It's much easier to act how we want to than to make a concerted effort to do the opposite of what everyone else does. We want others to treat us well, not judge us, and fully accept us for who we are, but we don't always want to extend that same favor to someone else. It's hard not to judge or to be nice to everyone we meet. It's our natural instinct to immediately "judge a book by its cover" and because we do that we usually miss out on the treasure contained within the story.

I've done my fair share of judging, but I've also had intense judgments directed at me. From strangers to family, I've felt the sting of being hard-core judged. Sometimes it's worse than a sting and cuts deep into my being.

I've been stopped by strangers in the mall who ask me if I know that a tube is hanging out of my body. I thank them and move on, trying not to contemplate their ignorance. They are referring to my IV tube and, believe it or not, I'm fully cognizant of the fact it's coming out of my shirt and looping back into the small backpack on my back, which holds the IV bag and pump.

I've had to reassure numerous strangers, doctors, friends, and family that I'm eating and not suffering from an eating disorder. Nevertheless, I still feel the stares of judgment enveloping me as people question the validity of my statement. I've lost friends because they've chosen to believe the judgmental statements they've created for themselves instead of the truth I tell them.

I've also experienced profound rejection from countless groups of people. Whether they are a church, sport, school or some other type of group, I've been ostracized because I'm different. It's complicated and frustrating to understand my disease. The things I have to do on a daily basis leave many wondering what exactly I go through. Many people get tired of being around someone who isn't getting better and I can feel the silent judgments they fling at me. I've never had someone explicitly tell me they don't want to hang out with me, but their actions speak much louder than any words they utter.

These silent judgments cut the deepest. Some piercing stares cut straight to my heart. Stares, which vocalize a much different story than the one emanating from their lips. Then there are others who subtly shun me until I stop trying to contact them. Everyone knows the silent rejection I speak of and I still haven't met someone who enjoys being the brunt of this.

Additionally, how many of us have chosen not to speak to or interact with someone because those around us have already deemed that person as "unpopular"? We wouldn't dare interact with them in case we too received that same label. If we attempted a conversation with this person, we feel extremely uncomfortable because we can sense the eyes of those around us, judging us because we've talked to the "unpopular" person.

Yet, while none of us likes to be judged or rejected, we all seem to dole it out. I'm not exempt. I wonder how many times I've seen someone and immediately decide I didn't want to deal with them. Before taking the time to get to know them, I immediately throw silent judgments at them with either my eyes, my actions or by some other means. I also come to conclusions about someone because I may not like how they act, talk or look. By doing this, I guarantee I've missed out on friendships. I've also failed because by choosing to ostracize them, I choose to not show them Jesus's love.

If you think about it, Jesus accepted everyone. No matter how ugly or broken, He showed them compassion and love. He chose to associate with the "unpopular" crowd and he didn't show any embarrassment when He talked to or touched these people. Whether they were a child or adult, affluent or destitute, a royal or beggar, a man or woman, He lavished love and acceptance on all. No one ever experienced the pain of rejection from Jesus and that's why He was loved by so many.

I've felt some of the worst rejection and judgment from "Christians." For a while, it made me want nothing to do with the church. I was confused when people who weren't "religious" showed me more love than those who I met at church. I know I'm not alone in feeling the harsh judgment and exclusion from Christians. I know many people who won't step foot in a church or bother to learn more about Jesus because of how they've been treated. This is a drastic misrepresentation of the heart of Jesus. Christians are humans just like the rest of us. While they may wish to emulate Jesus, they are human and make mistakes like everyone else. The mistakes they make are condemned at a higher level because we assume if they're Christians then they will act just like Jesus. While many of them diligently try to emulate their Savior, others falter and leave a bitter taste in the mouths of those they encounter. However, it seems when we picture Christians and the Christian church we imagine people who are stuck-up, judgmental, and full of hypocrisy. While these people are in the church, they aren't anywhere near an accurate representation of Jesus. Jesus loved and accepted the worst of humanity and He wasn't one to judge or reject someone, no matter how horrible they were.

Why can't we truly represent Jesus and His church? Why do we continue to judge others and push them into corners where they become abandoned? We do it for our own sense of security and worth. We go along with the crowd and treat others like we don't want to be treated so our peers who watch will treat us well. It's a conundrum slowly tearing our society and world apart. How many great conversations and friendships have we lost out on because we didn't want to show love to the person wearing last year's fashions? How many times could we have prevented depression to seep into someone's mind if we had only smiled at that person instead of barely glancing his or her way? How many times have we automatically assumed the person covered in tattoos and wearing dirty clothing is the culprit instead of the clean-shaven, nicely dressed person who is the real delinquent? How many lives have we not been able to touch because we chose to ignore the people that needed love the most? How often have we rejected others to save our own skin? As I ponder these questions, my soul is pained, because I know I've missed out on opportunities to change peoples' lives for the better.

Will we continue to judge, shun, and ignore those around us? Sadly, yes. We're not perfect and never will be. We will still make mistakes, hurt others, and treat them as we don't want to be treated. Yet, we can still strive to make an effort to truly follow the golden rule and adopt a heart like Jesus. It's not easy. It's much simpler to fall back into our old patterns, but in doing this we continue hurting others. We must make a concerted effort to abandon the old path we've traveled on and begin a new journey of striving to show love and acceptance to all.

This doesn't mean you have to be best friends with every single person you come into contact with. It means you'll talk to the one person in the room no one else talks to. It means you won't be afraid to be seen in public with someone who is "unpopular." It means you'll stick up for others who are picked on. When you want to reject someone, you'll instead include him or her. It means you'll stop judging people by their exterior and take a minute to learn who they are on the inside.

I pray daily I would have a heart like Jesus, but I won't ever have that heart if I can't accept "the least of these" (Matthew 25:40, NIV). God never called any of His creations a mistake; He considered all His creations His masterpieces.

Therefore, we need to start treating every individual as the masterpiece they are, not as the failure humanity wishes us to see them as. Will you decide to view others as a masterpiece? You may uncover treasures you never knew this person had. Your heart will change for the better. Most important, when you emulate the heart of Jesus you slowly change the stereotype the church has been labeled with. Maybe people will find the love and acceptance they crave, instead of the judgmental stares and rejection many have associated with Christians.

Hope

September 6, 2014

Hope. A simple four-letter word, which holds a powerful message. When you have it, you can conquer the world. When you've lost it, the world comes crashing down around you. It creates visions and puts them into action. It allows people to survive. It gives strength to those who've lost everything. It allows renewal to flow through populations. It allows rebirth and new growth. It brings strength to the weary. It pierces through the darkest moments life brings. It's strong and bold. It allows survival when survival seems impossible. It creates communities. It bolsters love. It brings peace. It's an emotion that can change the world.

Hope leaves the eyes of those who've given up their fight. Hopeless eyes are full of sorrow, guilt, shame, and regret. They are dull and vacant. Those without hope are lost in a dark and desolate forest. They are stuck in the murkiness of life and can't find a way out. They've given up, and soon the trials of life will bury them if they can't find hope again.

Those with hope don't give up. They push through obstacles others believe are immovable. They find a way to clamber out of the deep, dark holes of regret, sadness, and disappointment. They see a path where others see a wall. They find happiness in the little things. Peace radiates from them. Their eyes brilliantly shine because they know where there is a will there is a way. They may be sick, dying, poor, and destitute, but their countenance tells a story of health, life, wealth and happiness.

How do you find and keep hope? The search must start within you. You have to critically evaluate what has brought you hope in the past. If your hope lies in material things, then you'll lose it because you'll never be satisfied. If your hope lies in relationships, then you'll experience disappointment after disappointment because people aren't perfect. If your hope lies in emotions, then you'll ride a roller coaster for the rest of your life because emotions will always fluctuate. If your hope lies in your health, then you'll become hopeless because everyone experiences sickness. If your hope lies in the future, then you'll never experience it because the future you look toward will eventually become the present. In the present, you'll focus on what's next and miss the present moment. If your hope lies in success, you'll lose hope because at some point you'll fail. So where can you find hope?

The answer is simple. Stop looking for it. Hope is not something found. It's something already in all of us. We get caught up trying to find it, we miss that we already have it. What we choose to do with our hope is key. You see, so many of us put our hope in material things, health, relationships, the future, etc., but you won't experience hope in any of that. Why? Those things, at some time or another, will always bring some type of disappointment. So we're back to square one. Where do we put our hope?

There is only one secure place where we can put our hope. That place is in the hands of Jesus. We may be disappointed with God because we don't receive what we prayed for, but we don't realize what we prayed for may result in greater sadness if God had granted the request. Sometimes disappointments are the best gifts God could give us. Through them, we learn and grow. Looking back, I see how unanswered prayers or answered prayers, which were disappointing, saved me from the deep sorrow I'd have endured if my prayer been answered as I wanted it to be. No, I haven't seen this with every "unanswered" prayer. However, when I get to heaven, I know I'll laugh when God shows me how the prayers I prayed would've resulted in anguish.

When you place your hope in Jesus' hands, you must place it fully in His hands. If you try to keep some it, you'll never experience full hope. You must completely give it to Jesus, to be completely filled with hope. While placing your hope in Jesus' hands, you must trust He will *never* abuse your hope or turn your hope into disappointment. We're used to being let down, seeing our hopes dashed, and experiencing the bitter taste of disappointment. Yet, we must trust Jesus to guard, protect, and nurture our hope so we're filled to capacity with the hope that never runs out.

I used to look for hope in my own achievements or search for it in the praise of others. However, I never found hope in any of those places and experienced disappointment after disappointment. Through disappointment, I learned I placed my hope in the wrong areas. I needed to place my hope in Jesus' hands, but I know I didn't place all my hope there right away. I tried to place half of my hope in Jesus' hands and half in other things. In doing that, I still experienced the biting sting of disappointment and sorrow. Eventually, I placed all my hope in Jesus and I finally had found that indescribable hope mentioned in the bible. My hope wasn't found in people or places. Instead, my hope was found in Someone who could never be shaken. I still experienced disappointment, but it was always outlined with hope. I no longer felt completely destitute or alone. No matter what I faced, a quiet peace radiated through me.

Sometimes, I can't see the light at the end of the tunnel and feel surrounded by a murky darkness. Nevertheless, hope radiates through me, pushing back the darkness with a light so pure and true I never lose my footing. Hope echoes in the laughter I thought I'd lost. Hope reflects in my eyes, bringing a shine to them, many thought was gone for good. Hope allows me to see the joy in sadness, the peace in turmoil and the relief in the midst of pain.

My hope is held in hands with brutal scars, which were made when Jesus took the disappointments, trials, and sins of this world onto Himself, in order to, establish hope for all. I now know, my hope will never be safer anywhere else. The question remains: Where have you put your hope?

Forgiveness

September 9, 2014

One word, three syllables and eleven letters—forgiveness. A word that is much easier to say than to apply to our lives. This word can be difficult to come to terms with, but it carries freedom. A word we all want to be applied to us when we've been wronged, but something we hesitate to extend to others.

Forgiveness is easy to bestow on others when they are repentant and are sorry about the pain they've caused. However, forgiving someone who isn't sorry for what they did is a whole different ball game. How do we forgive the spouse, parent, family member, friend or stranger who has verbally or physically abused us? How do we forgive the person who walked out of our lives? How do we forgive betrayal? How do we forgive those who took what meant so much to us from us? How do we forgive someone who we think doesn't deserve even a sliver of our forgiveness?

What we do is stop asking how or why and start applying the principle. That's easier said than done, but once we do it, we experience freedom. In choosing not to forgive, we let them win. We let them succeed in damaging us even more than they did to begin with. Why? Choosing not to forgive is a breeding ground for bitterness, anger, and resentment. One act of not forgiving leads to another and another. Pretty soon you have enough moments, where you have chosen not to forgive others, that you could fill many acres of ground with them. These acres become fertile soil for dark seeds to be sown. Seeds sprouting into weeds, which can eventually suffocate us.

How can something as simple as not forgiving someone turn into something that could suffocate you? When you don't forgive someone, you hold onto whatever they did to wrong you. The longer you hold onto it, the more you think about it, and the angrier you become about it. You start to feel a deep resentment and bitterness toward the wrongdoer. You become fixated on what they did to you. This fixation can turn into an obsession. An obsession that could slowly change your life.

Deciding not to extend forgiveness to one person can lead you to stop forgiving more and more people. How? Bitterness and anger from the first event will grow and cause you to become less and less likely to forgive others. Bitterness and anger from one thing can expand, until these emotions begin to lace every event you encounter. It can be a good event or a bad event, but the weeds of bitterness and anger will be present and continue to multiply if you refuse to forgive others. As they grow, you'll be consumed with them and your life will continue going downhill from there. Your perspective on life will change and you'll lose trust in others, experience more conflict, and have trouble viewing life through a glass half full.

Others may not see the emotions swirling in you, but you'll sense them. Pride, arrogance, and a stubborn spirit will cause you to ignore the feelings or try to make excuses as to why it's acceptable for you to feel this way. If you continue to let them grow, they'll suffocate you. The laughter and peace once filling you will be replaced by scowls and rage. You'll feel as though a heavy weight has been placed on your shoulders and as time passes it will appear to increase in weight. You'll become impatient and it will seem as though everyone has a vendetta against you. Confusion and misery will be present and life will become depressing.

Is refusing to forgive worth all that? It may seem like it is if you've been deeply hurt, but it really isn't. Please believe me. Many of us look at forgiveness as something we're doing for someone else. In reality, we either help ourselves by forgiving someone or we hurt ourselves worse by refusing to forgive.

Your words of forgiveness carry no significance if they don't come from the heart. That person may think you've forgiven them, but you still reap the sorrows of not forgiving, if you don't forgive them in your heart. This is where you achieve true freedom. You must let go of whatever they did to you. I know it's hard. I know it hurts to let go. Nevertheless, do it, so you can be free. Stop thinking about what the other person did to you and let it go. The longer you think about it, the harder it will be to let it go.

You may think your situation is hopeless because you've been holding onto something for years, but you can still forgive them. They don't even have to know, but you'll know and that's what is important. Stop letting their wrongdoing control and ruin your life. Stop letting them win. Stop losing. Let it go. Let them go. Let what they did go. In return, the wound they made will heal and will no longer fester. The bitterness and rage will be uprooted and laughter and peace will fill your eyes.

Remember, you won't be the first person who has had to forgive them. When they hurt you, they also hurt Jesus. He forgave them, so follow His example. Ask for His help and forgive them too. Forgiveness is not an easy concept. It brings freedom, but it takes work and release on your part to obtain freedom. As they say, freedom is never free. It will be an endeavor to earn this freedom, but the sweet taste of victory will be well worth the toil.

Peace

September 14, 2014

Quiet and gentle, it enveloped me. Filling me with an indescribable sensation. It was a mixture of unadulterated joy, diminished tension, and perfect tranquility. It was a feeling I never wanted to lose and one that had taken long to develop.

It was peace. The peace of God, which truly does transcend all understanding (Philippians 4:7, NIV). It wasn't a peace I could create on my own. Actually, it's not a peace any of us are capable of creating. It comes from one source, and you can only obtain this peace when you fully surrender to God.

Throughout my life, I believed I had surrendered to God. I accepted Jesus into my heart, but I don't think I ever fully gave Jesus my entire heart. I like to be in control.

Giving full control to someone else goes against the core of my being. I had convinced myself I gave Jesus control, but my heart told a different story.

For in the depths of my heart, swirled emotions that were in no way, shape or form associated with Jesus. A whirlwind of anger, sadness, tension, bewilderment, depression, and anxiety etched paths through my heart, wreaking havoc anywhere they traversed. I was tense, on edge, and would react negatively when things didn't go according to my "perfect" plan.

When I was on my "A-game," I could hide that whirlwind from everyone, but when I was beaten down and weary, the whirlwind became visible to those who saw me. I would lash out at those closest to me. Anger and frustration would lace the tone of my voice. Sadness reflected from the depths of my eyes. I was a mess but chose to ignore it, because surrendering my entire life to someone else was unthinkable.

Fortunately, my stupidity did not blind me. I realized how my actions were negatively impacting the lives of those who surrounded me. My actions weakened the bonds I had with those I loved the most. They caused me to live a life not worthy of my calling (Ephesians 4:1, NIV). By God's grace, I saw how my refusal of surrender caused immeasurable damage, not only in my life, but also in lives of those I came into contact with.

I began to pray for a heart like Jesus's heart. Then I realized that I had jumped ahead of myself. In reality, I needed to first pray for a heart willing to have a heart like Jesus. A heart, which would surrender all of its desires and yearn to be more like Jesus. My heart had been ransacked by a whirlwind of negative emotions brought on by my own resistance. I wanted a heart willing to do anything God asked.

To be honest, I don't have that heart yet. I'm still praying for that heart. I still have issues with control. I still want my plans to go perfectly, but there has been a change.

The whirlwind is gone. A new light has replaced the sadness reflecting from my eyes. The majority of the time, my tone of voice is now woven with happiness, instead of anger and frustration. I feel full, not empty. I feel whole, not broken. I feel redeemed, not abandoned. The broken parts of my life have begun to be repaired and I am starting to feel whole again. I have been set free from the prison, which I created for myself. A prison that I pray I never enclose myself in again.

Have you surrendered or are you still building your prison? As you saw, I had convinced myself and others I had surrendered, but at the heart of the matter, I hadn't. Maybe you resonate with one of these three scenarios: 1. You have surrendered and experience the same peace I do. 2. You convinced yourself and others you surrendered, but that whirlwind is wreaking havoc on your life. 3. You haven't surrendered one bit and you know it. You're caught in a storm of unfathomable danger.

Unless you're part of scenario one, then you need to seriously think about the topic of surrender. If you fail to begin this introspection sometime soon, you'll only become more embroiled in your personal storm. A storm that could end your life.

Choose surrender today, so in the end you achieve freedom. Choose this day to be part of scenario one, so you're no longer tossed around in the storm raging inside you. Choose today who you will serve, but as for me, I will serve the Lord (Joshua 24:15, NIV).

Normal

September 25, 2014

Normal. One of the biggest jokes on the planet. What is normal? Do we even know? Who decides what's normal?

We create our own standards of normal based on how we've been raised or according to society's views of normal. We get comfortable in our phase of life and decide it's normal and anything different would be abnormal or unacceptable. By doing this, do we hurt ourselves and prevent healing, changing or maturing? You see, what we sometimes need to do is change our normal in order to heal.

If your normal is eating junk food, not exercising, and watching TV, then you won't be able to adopt a healthy lifestyle unless you change your standards of normal to reflect that. If you've accepted someone yelling at you or hitting you as normal, then you'll continue to be abused until you change your normal to reflect a relationship that's not abusive. If your normal shuts people out of your life and you deal with emotions alone, then you won't heal until you view normal as a life where you share your struggles with those you trust.

In order for me to heal properly, I can't view the current state of body as normal. I'm severely underweight. If I viewed this state as normal, then any weight gain would cause me to think I was overweight, when I wasn't. I wouldn't heal until I adjusted my normal to match the weight that is deemed normal based on my body structure.

Do you understand what I'm trying to say? Each of us needs to critically evaluate our lives and what we call normal. For what we call normal may be damaging our lives. We will *never* be able to heal

from this damage unless we first
change our standards of normal.

The next question: Does fear keep
you from adjusting your standards?
Are you comfortable with your
normal? Sometimes we become
comfortable with what we have
deemed as normal and become
hesitant to adjust our standards,
even though they're detrimental to
us. We've accepted the standards
of normal, which we've created for
ourselves, and since we're still
surviving, we're afraid of what will
happen if we adjust our normal.

Sometimes, even though we may
be surviving, we're heading toward
destruction. Unfortunately, our fear
prevents us from seeing the
destruction, which looms in front of
us. By the time we see it's too late.
When we reach this point, we
realize our mistake, but there is
nothing we can do. If we're
fortunate, we're only injured, but
sometimes we aren't so fortunate
and we're ruined.

Stop letting fear control you. Stop accepting the normal you've created, which, in turn, is hurting you. Stop ignoring that voice urging you to adjust your standards of normal. Stop merely surviving.

Live. Overcome the fear binding and controlling you. Be brave. Adjust your standards of normal so you can finally heal. I'll be honest with you it won't be easy. It will be terrifying. It will be extremely difficult. However, if you don't do something soon, you'll cause yourself more pain. You'll continue to deny yourself the peace you crave. You'll remain embroiled in anger and frustration.

Don't try to do it on your own. If you don't want to open up to those around you, at least open up to Jesus. His heart breaks as He sees you suffer, but He won't try to force Himself on you. If you reach out to Him, He will pull you into His embrace and fill you with the strength you can't possess on your own. This strength will fill you with the resolve to face your fears and adjust your standards of normal, and peace will take the place of the terror you feel. He will be there for you if you reach out to Him.

No, I haven't completely adjusted my standards of normal. I still fear amending some of the standards in my life. However, I'll never achieve complete peace and healing unless I change. It's hard. It's incredibly difficult. So, I call out to my Savior and He answers. He's pulled me into His strong arms and He pours His strength and peace into me. He gives me the resolve to not give in to fear and He helps me to make modifications to my definitions of normal. It's a long journey that I just started, but I pray I'll be able to successfully reach my destination.

Will you join me on this journey? Traveling with a companion is much more enjoyable than venturing out on my own. Together we can share each other's burdens and not have to be alone any longer. Who knows what treasures we'll discover? Together, by adjusting our standards of normal, we can begin to heal.

Purpose

October 8, 2014

At some point, we all wonder what our purpose is in life. People become disheartened because they aren't sure about their purpose. Others are ecstatic because they've figured out their purpose in this life.

People full of purpose are driven, determined, and dedicated. On the other hand, people lacking purpose are depressed, dejected, and discouraged. Clearly we all wish to belong to the former group. If we already belong to this group, how do we stay there? If we're part of the latter group, how do we join the first one?

The answer is simple. It lies with what your purpose is. If your purpose is to become rich and famous, then you'll remain part of the second group until you're satisfied with your level of wealth and success. If your purpose is to help others, then you'll end up in the second category when you're unable to assist people. If your purpose is to rule the world, then you'll also not belong to the first group until you've achieved this feat. I could go on, but my point is this: You'll become part of the second group if your purpose lies in things, statuses or achievements connected with the world we live in.

Instead, your purpose should lie in God and not in the people or things of this world. When your purpose is focused on something in this world or on the people of this world, then you'll be on a roller coaster of emotions. When things, events, and moments seem to contribute to your "purpose," then you'll feel full of drive, determination, and dedication. However, when everything seems to conspire against you and nothing is going in the direction of your "purpose" then you'll feel depressed,

dejected, and discouraged.
Anything connected with the world
we live in will fail or disappoint us
at some point. This world is not
perfect. Therefore, if our "purpose"
lies within this world we will never
be completely happy. This is why
our purpose must lie outside of this
world.

I believed, from a young age that
my "purpose" in life was to go to
school and ultimately receive the
training required to work in the
medical field. I believed my
"purpose" was to help the hurting.
As I became sicker, I
simultaneously became
discouraged because the "purpose"
I'd determined for my life seemed
to slip away from me. I wasn't able
to enter Physician Assistant (PA)
school right after my
undergraduate career, like I had
planned. When I recently received
acceptance to a PA program, I had
to request they allow me to defer
until the next year because
currently I am unable to begin PA

school, due to my health issues. When I first learned that I wouldn't be able to go to PA school straight out of undergrad, I became depressed and dismayed. I wondered what my purpose was in life if I wasn't working toward my dream of belonging to the medical field. I realized that I would continue to feel useless if my purpose in life didn't change. In order for me to crawl out of the discouraged slump I was in, my purpose needed to stem from a source that wasn't connected to this world.

My purpose needed to be placed in the hands of God. Instead of praying I'd be able to get into this PA program or that PA program, I prayed I'd be able to fulfill the purpose God had deemed for my life. I started to ask Him to change my heart and my focus, so they were in line with His purpose. I requested He use me for the purposes He chose, instead of asking for His help in achieving the "purposes" I had picked. Guess what? Slowly, my attitude and outlook on life began to change. I became determined, driven, and dedicated to pursuing God's purpose for my life.

Do I know what His purpose is for my life? No. Do I know how my life will end up? No. Do I know what the future holds? No. Guess what? I don't need to know the answer to any of those questions to remain determined, driven, and dedicated. I only need to focus on staying attune to God's signals and progressing in the direction He has planned for me. This new path, toward God's purpose for my life, is riddled with confusion, questions, and worry. As long as I keep my eyes on Jesus, these things will merely pass me by and not remain attached to me.

I live in this world, a world that contains negative emotions like depression, anxiety, sadness and frustration. Therefore, I will still experience and be susceptible to these emotions. However, they will only remain a part of me if I make my purpose in life something of this world. As long as I accept that God has already determined the perfect purpose for my life and if I trust that He will never lead me astray, then those emotions will be fleeting. They will be strong and may feel overwhelming, but they'll pass.

I'm on a new journey. The destination is heaven, but I have no idea what the journey holds. I don't know if I'll ever be a PA. I don't know if I'll get married or have a family. I do not know if I'll live for five more years or fifty more. However, I do not need to know any of this. My type A personality doesn't like to accept this statement, but the declaration still remains true. *I do not need to know my future or purpose.* I only need to ask God to use me in His perfect plan and He will do that. However, I need to be ready to accept that whatever happens in my life is according to His plan, even if that thing seems horrible or overwhelming or I receive an answer I hadn't hoped for.

Typing this out is a lot easier than actually living it out. I like knowing how plans will be executed. I like to have a clear destination in place. I don't like upsets (unless it's the Florida Gators upsetting a rival). I don't like change. I don't like the answers "no" or "wait". However, I'm learning to accept all those things I don't like. Man, it's hard. It's scary. So far, it has given me a new drive in life. I'm not as discouraged, dejected, and depressed as I once was. This alone tells me I'm walking along a better life path. I may not be moving quickly. I may even stumble along, but I'm still making forward progress.

Will you ask God to lead you in the purpose He has for your life? Will you stop trying to pursue "purposes" rooted in a world where all things will come to an end at some time or another? Will you become blind to your life journey so you see and experience the peace and hope God seeks to give? Will you take a leap of faith so you'll one day hear, "Well done my good and faithful servant"? (Matthew 25:21, NIV).

Fear

October 13, 2014

Ice-cold tendrils of fear threaded their way through my body. I tried to grapple with them, but they were deft and crafty in their movements and managed to evade my searching fingers. They threaded their way through my entire being and melted into me. Their ghostly strands took on the form of my flesh, making it impossible for me to decipher where they lay. I was under attack from an enemy whose disguise was my own skin, and I was powerless to hamper fear's hold on me; powerless if I tried to tackle it on my own.

Since the latter part of the spring and the entire summer of 2012, fear has been a constant companion. Fear of becoming locked in the torture chamber of pain, bloating, and nausea that accompanied each meal. Fear of not being able to escape.

In 2012, when I was at a healthy weight, I thought my body looked much better than it does now. I also loved the new energy I had. Nevertheless, I began to dread meals. I dreaded them because I didn't want to experience the pain, bloating, and nausea, which occurred after the meals. The terrible trifecta became my own personal torture chamber, sending me into physical and mental anguish. It was too overwhelming to deal with. Sometimes I would vomit and it would release me from the personal hell I was embroiled in. Other times I wouldn't vomit and I would be locked in that chamber for hours on end.

Now, I believe a new pattern has developed, because I think my body learned that vomiting was the key, which unlocked my torture chamber. Our bodies are wired with various protective mechanisms so we can be saved from dangerous things. For example, if you ingest a substance that has gone bad or you've been poisoned, you'll experience pain, bloating, vomiting, and nausea, because your body recognizes it needs to get out whatever foul thing is inside you, become seriously ill or die. Therefore, my theory is that part of my vomiting is due to the fact that food always triggers pain, nausea, and bloating in me. It's a protective mechanism against this dreadful trifecta. My body rejects the food and I vomit so I won't be locked in that torture chamber for hours on end.

Intertwined throughout the foundation of this protective mechanism are those tendrils of fear. Not only do I consciously fear being locked in my torture chamber, but I also believe fear is interwoven into my subconscious. The fear brought on by the damaging trifecta elicits anxiety and panic. All of which contribute in some way or another to the vomiting.

It is a fear I must face, but one I know I can't face alone. Fortunately, I've learned that I don't need to fear, even if I'm walking through the valley of the shadow of death, aka my proverbial torture chamber. He (Jesus) is with me. His rod and His staff will comfort me (Psalm 23:4, NIV). By relying on Him, I find courage to attempt another meal. Through His strength, I'm able to try again. By His fortitude, I press on. For I know I couldn't do it alone.

This binding fear is difficult to admit that I have. No one likes to recognize a fear that they harbor deep in the core of their being. No one likes to confess a weakness, which leaves them paralyzed, distraught, and discouraged. However, without acknowledging a fear ensnaring you, you allow the fear's roots to become stronger and embed themselves deeper into you. The fear controls you until it possesses you. In order to defeat the fear, the first step is to recognize that the fear is there. Confess it's vice in your life. Admit you need to overcome it. Then put action to your words. For words carry no weight when there is no follow through.

Once you've admitted having a fear that binds you, let someone else know. It's impossible to obliterate a fear on your own. You may think you can handle it by yourself, but without adequate support, your attack may backfire. Without backup, the fear may overwhelm and destroy you.

Defeating fears, especially ones that have existed for a long time, will be a slow process. The fear didn't grow and become established overnight. It will be a long and painful journey to overcome the fear that resides within you. Before you become discouraged, take a second and imagine the freedom you'll experience once the fear has been uprooted. A freedom you've allowed to slip from you because you're too afraid to confront the deeply engrained fear within. Don't allow the fear to win. Don't believe the lies it stealthily whispers into your ears. Don't accept your prison because you've learned how to make it comfortable. Don't settle, when you can fight. This is a battle that will cost so much if you lose, but will hold a great reward if you win. Every battle contains sacrifices. You'll have to sacrifice your comfort, your security, and yourself in order to purge the fear that is interwoven into your being. However, the sacrifice will be worth it because you'll save yourself from the doom you're headed toward.

Jesus's rod and staff comfort me. He leads me through my valley of the shadow of death. Jesus has shown me I need only to fear God. Jesus is there for me. Don't worry, He's the world's best multitasker, so while He's doing all that for me,

He can also do it for you, just ask Him. I guarantee that's one person you won't regret asking for help. Talk to others whom you trust. Find professionals who have made it their life's work to help people uproot whatever fear binds them. Form a team so you're not alone. For alone you're easily defeated, but where many stand together victory is close at hand.

Start today. Recognize your fear. Admit that you need to defeat it. Ask for Jesus's help. Confess you have this fear to others. Begin to free yourself from the fear that binds you. Then experience the freedom that will come as the fear slowly begins to dissipate.

Burden

October 22, 2014

Every step was harder than the last. Salty sweat bathed his entire body. It was tinged red from the blood that poured from numerous wounds. This salty mixture dripped into His eyes, causing them to burn profusely. The heavy beam, from which He would hang, weighed heavily on his shoulders and dug into the freshly ravished flesh of His back. He could still feel the torturous sting from the Roman whip. White bone was visible around His rib cage where His flesh had been ripped off. Pinpricks of pain reverberated around His skull from the gruesome crown of thorns He bore. He was worn, beaten, and utterly exhausted.

He suddenly stumbled over a small rock and fell to the worn dirt path. The beam rolled off His shoulders and He cried out in agony. A soldier prodded at Him with His spear, but He was too weak to pick up the limb again. He lifted His head to meet the soldier's eyes and He saw eyes full of anger, confusion and a touch of sadness. The soldier turned to the crowd and grabbed a man, they called Simon, from the throng. The soldier ordered Simon to pick up the heavy beam and carry it for Jesus. Wearily, Jesus stood again and began anew His trek to Golgotha. He was thankful He didn't have the burden of the beam any longer and silently prayed for strength to finish the mission He'd been given.

"As they were going out, they met a man from Cyrene, named Simon, and they forced him to carry the cross" (Matthew 27:32, NIV).

One verse. Twenty-one words. Yet, too often we skim over it, writing it off as a random detail added to the story of Jesus's crucifixion. We fail to grasp the powerful significance of these twenty-one words. The lesson demonstrated in this verse is simple but extremely profound. It shows even Jesus had help carrying His burden. Take just a minute to let that sink in. Jesus. The Savior of the world. The all-mighty. The all-powerful. Even He had help carrying His burden.

Don't you see? If the Redeemer of the world, the Prince-of-Peace, the Mighty King, had help carrying His burden, don't you think this shows us we shouldn't try to carry our burdens alone? We should allow someone else to help us carry this burden. You may point out that the soldiers forced Simon to carry Jesus's cross. It wasn't like Jesus asked for help, but I believe this is actually a display of God's love. God doesn't want any of us to carry our burdens alone. God knew Jesus needed help, but Jesus couldn't ask for it because Jesus had no say against the soldiers. God had the soldiers force Simon to carry the cross. For God doesn't want anyone carrying their burdens by themselves, and if you can't give it up yourself, He'll provide a means for someone else to help you. Jesus could've refused to let Simon carry the cross, but Jesus knew He really couldn't carry His burden by himself.

We come back to the original question; if Jesus needed help to carry His burden, don't you think this means we all need help in carrying our burdens? The answer is a glaring yes, but too many of us say no. Pride keeps us from sharing our burdens with anyone else. We appear strong, capable, and in control. We may succeed at putting up this facade, but on the inside we're weak, vulnerable, and chaos is rampant. It's easy to ask someone to share in a physical burden; like grocery bags, household chores, yard work, work assignments, etc. On the other hand, it's incredibly difficult to share with some an emotional or psychological problem. In the later case, we'd have to admit that we needed help with something someone didn't even realize we struggled with. We'd have to be transparent, and transparency is incredibly difficult in an opaque world.

However, if Simon didn't carry Jesus's cross then Jesus may have not completed His journey to Golgotha, where Jesus's life work was accomplished. Did you catch this second hidden message? If we don't allow people to help us with our burdens, we may not successfully complete the mission we were placed here on earth to fulfill. In failing to share your burden with someone else, you may fail to fulfill the purpose God has for you.

There is a third subtle message contained within these twenty-one words. Sometimes your burden may be a component of your life mission. The cross, an incredibly painful and overwhelming burden, was a crucial component of Jesus's mission on earth. He died on the cross so we might have freedom. His greatest burden became His greatest gift. Likewise, the biggest burdens in our life may be critical elements of the mission we were called to fulfill on earth. Our heaviest burdens may be the ones we utilize to impact others. Our deepest sorrows may lead to overwhelming happiness in someone else's life. Our greatest heartaches may mend other people's broken hearts.

It all begins with us. We have to make the choice to share our burdens with someone else or, if we don't, their weight will become unbearable. I'm not saying it's easy. I'm not saying it's painless. I'm not saying it's a quick process. I'm saying it's worth it. If Jesus couldn't carry His burden alone, then neither can we. If He couldn't do it, then we surely shouldn't even try to. You see if the only person who can defeat the devil can't carry their burden alone, then how can we possibly think we can?

I'm the type of person who likes to carry my burdens myself. I don't like to admit when I'm weak or struggling. I don't like to admit when I'm scared, frustrated or feeling alone. When I swallow my pride and put aside my fear that I will be judged or when I ask for help, the weight on my shoulders is easier to bear. It doesn't mean my burdens disappear, it just means I don't have to carry them alone.

Take a step back and contemplate the burdens you carry. Find someone you trust and ask them to help you carry your burden. By holding onto your burden alone, you may prevent yourself from accomplishing the mission God has for you on earth. Remember, your burden may be an intricate part of that mission. Without your burden, you may never complete your assignment. Trust in God's perfect will. You may never know the reason for your burden until you get to heaven, but know you were given it for a reason. Without it, you may not have been able to touch the hearts you already have, or be able to touch other hearts in the future. Remember Jesus words, "I have told you these things, so in me you may have peace. In this world you will have trouble. But take heart! I have overcome the world." (John 16:33, NIV).

Sacrifice

November 5, 2014

"Slap" the sound of the squeegee making contact with the shower tile echoed throughout my bathroom. I drew the squeegee down, removing excess water from the wall. "Slap" I made contact with the wall again and repeated the process over and over again until all the water droplets had been scraped from the tile. The threat of mold and mildew building up was once again diminished. After I had hung the squeegee on the wall, I grabbed my towel and wrapped it around my body, letting the soft cloth envelop me and chase the cold away.

I absolutely hate having to squeegee the tile in my shower, but I have to do it to prevent damage to the shower. Technically, I could avoid using the squeegee, but it would mean I wouldn't be able to take a shower. Taking a nice hot shower is something I look forward to each night because it brings me comfort, peace and heavenly warmth. In the end, the joy and pleasure from the shower outweighs the frustration and annoyance of having to squeegee down the shower walls.

This just goes to show that if you aren't willing to make small sacrifices, you may never be able to enjoy something that could bring you pleasure and happiness. If I wasn't willing to deal with the frustration of having to squeegee down the shower tiles, then I wouldn't be able to experience the pleasure of taking a shower. Of course, I could avoid squeegeeing the tiles, but then I'd have a bigger problem on my hands. I'd have to scrub the mold and mildew from my shower. There are two lessons we can learn from this simple shower.

First, to achieve the greatest things out of life you need to be willing to make sacrifices. Unfortunately, we allow fear, selfishness or laziness stop us from making these crucial sacrifices. Fear of rejection or retaliation prevents us from moving out of our comfort zones and meeting new people or trying new things. Wanting more things for ourselves stops us from giving to others and missing out on the joy and satisfaction of blessing someone else. Disdain for work or making an effort inhibits our ability to obtain a raise or promotion in our job or better grades at school. In essence, we miss out on things that could make our life better because we are unable to make a sacrifice, which pales in comparison to the reward.

What sacrifices are you avoiding? What are you missing out on? At times, you may also have to sacrifice good things in order to obtain something even better. In order to build relationships, you have to sacrifice your time. However, time seems to be worth more than gold these days and relationships suffer because people value monetary investments more than personal ones. This mistake is deadly. We place such a high value on remaining financially stable we don't want to sacrifice work to make time for others.

Many times when we're asked how we're doing, the most popular response seems to be; *I'm good, just busy.* It's a gut response, but is it one that we truly consider? We want to be busy because maybe we're making more money or doing more things. Nevertheless, have we considered the toll it has on our lives? When our bodies don't get the rest they need, they become worn down and we become sick, depressed, anxious, angry, etc. Are we willing to sacrifice some of our "busyness" in order to achieve peace, health, happiness, etc.?
 The roots of busyness may stem from work, sports, extracurricular activities, and friendships. Not all causes of busyness are necessarily bad things. Therefore, sometimes

we must sacrifice good things to achieve even better things. Unfortunately, we're often blinded by what we're doing in the moment that we refuse to make the sacrifice. We refuse to take the rest we need and before we know it, it's too late and our body shuts down. This can come in the form of a cold or flu, a panic attack, a heart attack or many other dangerous things.

With that in mind, will you let fear, selfishness or laziness prevent you from making the necessary sacrifices to achieve even greater things? Will you keep going in the same deadly manner until your body shuts down? Will you blind yourself to the truth because you find denial easier than being honest and admitting you need to make critical sacrifices in your life? How will you answer these questions?

The second lesson we learn from the shower is when we don't make the small sacrifices we have to deal with bigger problems. Sometimes these big problems also require a lot of outside help to solve. I hinted at this above, by saying if you don't sacrifice some of your busyness you might end up with a serious health or relationship problem on your hands. Back to my original example, if I still take a shower, but don't squeegee down the tiles, I may have a major mildew and mold problem that has to be dealt with. If I wait too long, I'll have to call a professional to clean everything out. In the meantime, while the mold and mildew build I may start to suffer health complications from the buildup. Then I would have to see a doctor so I could take care of the health repercussions. However, if I had made small sacrifices in the beginning and squeegeed the tiles right after my shower, I wouldn't have to deal with the repercussions from a mold and mildew overgrowth.

The same goes for life—if we make the small sacrifices, like sacrifice busyness for peace, or our time to build a relationship, or study more to make better grades, we can reap huge rewards. However, if we don't make sacrifices we could end up with serious consequences. If we didn't sacrifice our busyness we could have a heart attack, which, in turn, would put us behind in whatever we're trying to accomplish. It could even grace us with expensive medical bills or death. If we don't sacrifice our time to build and nurture relationships, we might end up friendless or spouseless. If we don't sacrifice fun times in order to study, we may end up without a degree. When you look at it in this light, those small sacrifices are surely worth their cost because if we don't make them, we'd end up with much costlier situations on our hands.

You may think you're special or smart and you can find a way around making those sacrifices. You may say those "bad things" only happen to people who don't plan right. In reality, you're making excuses and trying to find a way out of the inevitable. Don't pursue this route, because it's bound to end in failure and this failure, could be extremely costly. Please don't let your cockiness kill you.

Sacrifices aren't easy that's why they're called a sacrifice. Some sacrifices are extremely difficult to make while others are a piece-of-cake. Most of the time, they are well worth the cost. If the sacrifice seems too big to deal with, don't give up, but also don't try to handle it alone. Jesus waits for you to ask Him for help; so ask and it will be given to you (Matthew 7:7, NIV). Also, seek out professional help if you need to. I know negative stigmas are associated with seeking help from a counselor, psychologist or psychiatrist, but these stigmas are stupid, wrong and causing people to harm themselves. If you need help from one of these sources, get it before you cause more damage to yourself. The whole world doesn't need to know about it, actually no one does, but you may be surprised by the freedom that comes from telling those you trust and love that you are struggling, but are obtaining help in overcoming the problem.

Take a moment to reflect on the sacrifices you need to make in your life so that you can meet new people, do new things, find more peace, experience profound pleasure, become full of happiness, etc. Don't let lies, frustration, fear, laziness, or anything else prevent you from making the sacrifices you know you need to make. It's a new journey to embark on and one you definitely shouldn't delay or avoid.

Depression

November 13, 2014

Dread, doubt, and disgust wormed their way into my brain. Anxiety, grief, and loneliness seeped through my pores into my bloodstream, traversing their way through my system. Bewilderment, frustration, and disappointment clawed their way to my heart. Each emotion intertwined with the others, their tendrils extending to form a thick fog of depression settling over my entire being. Its damp presence cruelly suffocated me, forcing me to become hopeless, disoriented, and distraught. My heart felt heavy, exhaustion overwhelmed my brain, tears threatened to overflow from my eyes. Yet, on the outside, all others saw was a smiling face and blue eyes only slightly tinged with pain and sadness. A girl who appeared tired, but otherwise normal. No one else could see the thick fog surrounding her. The fog that threatened to overpower her at any moment.

Depression. The silent disease. The illness few choose to address or confront, and because of this it spirals out of control. It carries stigmas which are utterly wrong and absolutely terrifying. These stigmas cause others to deny their suffering, and they attempt to hide it in any way they can. However, the longer it remains hidden, the faster it grows, and the farther you disappear into the fog.

Let me say something radical. Depression is normal. Normal in the sense that there is nothing wrong with experiencing those feelings. However, if you don't address those feelings, then they fester and spiral out of control. This is where normal becomes dangerous and when those festering feelings need to be addressed before you're pushed over the edge. Most people have experienced, are experiencing or will experience feelings of depression at some point or another in their life. Losing a sports match, getting a bad grade, experiencing an illness, working through grief, etc. all arouse feelings of depression. You're human so you're bound to experience these emotions. However, it's what you do with these feelings that determine the outcome of the depression.

Do I like admitting I struggle with depression? Absolutely not! I like others to believe that the smiling, confident, optimistic girl they interact with is a direct reflection of the girl inside. I tell people I have rough days and I wonder why I should keep fighting. I say that I get discouraged and depressed. Even when I admit these things, some people have trouble believing me, because my exterior doesn't hint at the feelings brewing on the inside.

It's true. I do struggle with depression, self-doubt, and anxiety. Half the time I wonder why I bother to keep fighting and the other half I wondering if I'm truly fighting with everything I have. I wonder if I've become comfortable with where I am because I've learned how to manage my life as I know it. I wonder if I'm too afraid to implement radical changes because I'm not sure what these changes will bring. I question if I've lost control over my disease and instead let it control me. I overthink. I overanalyze. Yet, deep down I know there is a thread of truth in the statements I've uttered. A thread that I wish wasn't there.

If that thread exists, I must start to change. Change is absolutely terrifying, overwhelming, and difficult when you've learned to accept the life you're living. Through acceptance, you've learned to manage whatever you're dealing with that you resist change. You don't want to learn how to manage something new.

You already feel like you're dangling from an enormous cliff by a thin string. If you fall, you'll land in a prickly briar patch. You cling to that thin string for dear life and you're afraid to move a muscle because you don't want that string to snap. It's a terror that paralyzes your body. Even if people are at the top of the cliff shouting at you to try this or that, you don't want to attempt anything because you don't want to risk falling. Terror freezes your senses and makes you numb. You're blind to solutions that may seem obvious to others. Solutions that could rescue you from the threat of falling, but solutions you're too terrified to try. You don't want to do anything to risk the precarious situation you are in.

Most of the time people don't understand how frozen you are by fear and depression. They judge and criticize you for not attempting solutions that seem so easy and obvious to them. They fail to put themselves in your shoes and their judgment and criticism only cause you to become more withdrawn and subdued. As you become more withdrawn, people judge you with more vehemence, and a disastrous cycle is formed until you shut everyone out of your life. You do this because you don't know how else you'll remain sane. What happens when you shut others out? The depression grows and you wonder why you even bother to cling to your thin string, because falling and giving up seem like the easiest options at this point.

Have I ever thought about letting go of my string? Absolutely. Have I ever let go? Yes. Why am I still here? It's because when I let go, Jesus grabbed my hand and said, "Not yet, my child, I haven't called you home, so don't try to come before I do so." He then placed my hands back on the string and said, "Hold on my child and look at the people above you." When I looked up, I saw a crowd milling about.

Many weren't really paying attention to me. They'd shout encouragement and check on my progress, but they had many other things occupying their time. However, I noticed three faces whose focus was solely on me. Their eyes held enormous pain for they didn't want to lose me. If I strained, I could hear their words of love and encouragement. I could also see their prayers wafting over their heads to heaven. The eyes that I gazed into belonged to my family. My family who had resolved not to give up on me, even when I wanted to give up on myself. I realized that by letting go, I'd bring pain to every single person in that crowd and worst of all I'd destroy my family. I took a deep breath and I tightened my grip on my string.

Am I still dangling? Yes. Am I planning on letting go anytime soon? No. Am I still assaulted by depression, fear, and anxiety?

Definitely. Will I be drowned by those emotions? No.

I've prayed for the last few months for God to work on my heart. For God, to show me where I allow fear to overpower me, where I succumb to depression and how I let my disease control me. True to form, He has answered. I wanted Him to say to me, You aren't letting fear dominate you. Depression isn't close by. You aren't letting your disease control you. Nevertheless, His answer was a little different. An answer I need to accept and address. An answer I need help in solving. So right now, I'm taking baby steps because right now those are the only ones I can take.

Do you need to take baby steps in your life? Does fear cause you to be frozen? Is depression threatening to suffocate you? Are you contemplating letting go of your string? Take your eyes off the briar patch. Look up. Don't focus on the fall or the bottom. Think about the treasures, rewards, and successes that lie at the top of that cliff and dare to make the changes necessary so you aren't clinging to your string anymore.

Change can't come if you choose to confront it alone. We think we're capable of handling our own problems, but in reality we aren't. We can't achieve the same measure of success, we're unable to reach the same goals, and we cannot confront the emotions we need to, if we attempt to do it alone. It's hard to ask for help, admit you're struggling, and acknowledge you're not in a good place, but once you do it, you can begin the path of healing. You can't embark on this path without first finding someone to help you on your journey. Pray and ask for God's help, but also find a person or multiple people to help guide and support you as you begin your baby steps. This may include parents, siblings, friends, counselors, psychologists, doctors, etc., but you can't tackle it alone or say, "I only need God to help me." That's the easy and wrong answer. Challenge yourself. Stop accepting the life you're living when you know change is critical.

Acknowledgements

First and foremost I want to thank God for giving me the insight and inspiration for the words found within these pages. I want to thank Him for carrying me through each and every day as I continue to fight my battle. I also want to express my gratitude to Him for giving me this battle to fight. Many may think it's strange that I thank Him for the thing that brings me the most pain and anguish, but by His graciousness I have been able to transform this burden into a gift for others. I have a passion for helping those who are hurting because I know what it's like to hurt. I have developed a fascination for the medical field, partly because I have grown up going to hospitals and seeing doctors. I have been able to help people I never would have had the opportunity to touch, if I hadn't suffered first. I have had the opportunity to teach classes, be on the news and in newspapers because of my battle. So you see, what many see as a curse from God, I see as a blessing in disguise because I have been able to use my disease to bring hope to others.

Secondly I want to thank my family. We surely aren't perfect. We definitely have our flaws. But we love each other with an undying love. We fight for each other. We pray for each other. We stick together through thick and thin and that's what makes us strong. It took me until college to learn the true value of my family, but once I did I began to thank God every day for them, for without them I wouldn't be alive.

To my wonderful father, Tim Fox. I've always been a daddy's girl. I am his princess. He is my king. He has promised to guard my heart until the day another man is worthy enough to accept this duty. My father has loved me from the day I was born and has never stopped. With a degree in engineering, health stuff can be incredibly overwhelming for him, but that doesn't stop him from working extra hard to understand what the doctors are saying about me. He's never hesitated to put my needs above his career. He has taken me to numerous doctors' appointments and patiently waited with me through ER visits or different procedures I've undergone. I remember one bleak, dreary day this past February when I decided that I no longer wanted to fight. When I stubbornly announced I no longer wanted to be kept alive by artificial things and I just wanted to go home to Heaven. I spent the entire day, sitting on the floor of my room staring blankly at the wall. Instead of becoming upset or frustrated with me, my dad just came and sat on the floor by me and said nothing. He just sat there so I wouldn't be sitting alone. If that's not love, I don't know what is.

To my amazing mother, Cynthia Fox. You have the strength that many mothers merely dream of possessing. You have lived a life that for many other mothers is there worst fear, but has never become reality. Yet you've lived this life with such grace and strength. I am never scared to go to the doctors or undergo a new test because you are always there right by my side. When I turned 18 you didn't stop accompanying me to doctor's appointments or ER visits, instead you left the choice up to me and when I asked if you'd still come, you didn't hesitate to say yes. You've traveled with me around the country, as we go to hospital after hospital and you've never complained. You are first and foremost my mother, but recently you've also been my nurse and I couldn't have requested a better nurse than you! I asked you the other day if you'd be able to get your shift at work covered for when we had to take another trip. Your response was, "If I can't get something worked out, then I can just quite, because it's not as important as you are." That response touched me in ways you'll never know. Your love keeps my heart beating.

To my incredible little brother, Kevin Fox. I seriously don't know what I would do without you in my life. You're the pesto to my pasta, the butter to my biscuit, the foam to my coffee, the beat to my heart. I seriously cherish each and every minute I get to spend with you and you give me more support than you'll ever realize. This past year when I was in the hospital, even though you were extremely busy with school, an internship, work and normal day to day things, you took the time to come to the hospital and sit and talk to me for a little while. You were exhausted, since you'd barely slept the night before, but instead of taking a nap, you sacrificed your time to visit me and bring a smile to my lips. Last year when you came to my graduation at the University of Florida, right before you left I asked you if you'd enjoyed your visit since we were able to go out to midtown and were able to experience the "party" side of Gainesville. I'll never forget your response. You told me that you didn't come here to party. You came there to watch me walk and if that's the only thing you'd done the whole trip you'd still have been happy. So, thank you little one for supporting me through my ventures. For fighting for me when I've thought I couldn't fight any longer. For supporting me physically, emotionally and spiritually. For physically sharing Psalm 139 with me. I am beyond blessed to have you in my life and am honored to call you my brother. I love you to the moon and back. "If you live to be a hundred, I want to live to be a hundred minus one day so I never have to live a day without you."- Winnie the Pooh.

To my mom's family: Grandma; Uncle Brian & Shari; Uncle Kevin & Aunt Joanne; Uncle Michael & Aunt Ruth Ann; Uncle Jimmy; Uncle Mike, Aunt Eileene, Kim & Alyson; Aunt Carolyn, Katrina & Marci; and Aunt Kathleen. Thank you for the love and support you've sent me and continue to send me. You brighten my days and help me to continue to push on in my fight.

To my dad's family: Uncle Mike, Aunt Donna, Zack & Joseph; and Uncle Jim, Aunt Karen, Cait, Kyleigh, Nate & Candace. You all have stuck by my side through my entire battle. Loving me, caring for me and sending me things to keep my spirits high. Thank you from the bottom of my heart.

To the Snow Mountain Gang: Uncle John & Aunt Kay; Sam, Mary, John, Jenny & Jessie; Teresa, Henry, Margo, Madeline & Matthew; Becky, Kaitlyn, Kyle, Amanda & Mike; and Annie. I may not be a first relative to any of you all, but each and every one of you have accepted me and loved me in a way that I could never imagine. Thank you for the impact you've made on my life.

To Grandma and Grandpa Kenaston. Once again I am able to publish a book because of how you all have supported me financially. But even more important than that you've supported me through prayers and love, something that is truly priceless. Thank you Grandma Kenaston for faithfully editing all my essays. They wouldn't flow as nicely if not for your dedication and hard work in editing each and every one of them.

To Grandma and Grandpa Huffman. Your continuous stream of letters, cards and care packages are always a bright spot in the midst of my dreary days. Sometimes I'll wait to open your letters until there comes a time when I especially need my spirits lifted and you never disappoint.

To the Garrity's (Papa Bill and Granna). Wow you guys are amazing prayer warriors and I am so blessed to have you in my life. You've supported and encouraged me through cards, special gifts and love. God blessed me richly when He placed you guys in my life. Don't ever underestimate the power of your prayers, for He does listen and He does answer, so don't ever stop praying. I know when you guys get to the gates of Heaven, you'll hear, "Well done my good and faithful servants."

To my Great Aunt Kay and Great Uncle John. Thank you for the blessing you've been in my life. I love being pen pals with you Aunt Kay and I am so honored that you faithfully write to me even when we live so close to each other.

To Granddad and Tommy. Although you guys may not be here on earth anymore, you'll forever live in my heart. You two made an incredible impact on me in the short time span I knew you and I will never forget your undying love, care and concern for others.

To Dr. Rogers. You've been the most incredible doctor that I can ever imagine. I wish that every future doctor could train under you so that they could fully understand and grasp the importance of treating their patients like a person and not a chart. Your faithful care for me has touched me deeper than you'll ever know and I can never begin to thank you. I love you so much Dr. Rogers and I'm so blessed to have you in my life.

To Angie Francis. I was nervous when they told me I was getting a new nurse case manager, but you've gone above and beyond in your job and you've hardly disappointed me. Thank you for all your hard work and dedication.

To Cynthia Clare. Thank you for being such a wonderful home

healthcare nurse case manager. I am beyond blessed to know you and have you as a nurse in my life. The genuine care and concern you show for your patients, touches them in ways you'll never realize. Love you so much!

To Zack Fox. Sure we may be cousins, but you've become more than just a cousin to me, you've become one of my best friends. You are such an amazing man. I've always joked that I'd be dating you if you weren't my cousin and I think that alone says what an incredible man you are. Thank you for always encouraging, calling and texting me. I cherish all our conversations and the times I get to spend with you. We've made many memories together and I can't wait to make more.

To Nicole White. You are one of my best friends and I am so honored that you've given me the gift of your friendship. I will never forget the things you've done for me and all that you continue to do for me. To you, it doesn't matter that miles now separate us. You still text me and love me from afar. You will always have a very special place in my heart.

To Meghan Neary. You too are one of my best friends. I cherish our daily texting conversations. I appreciate that we can be honest with each other and give each other solid advice. When you visited me in the summer of 2014 that was by far one of the best weeks of my summer. Then after my long month at Mayo in June 2015 you surprised me the day after I came back. God surely worked that out, but you will never truly know how much that visit meant to me. I still think I dreamed it and I can't wait until the day I get to see you again. You too will always hold a special place in my heart.

To Sarah Sarnoski. To you it doesn't matter that we barely see each other or that we've lived in separate states for the past two years. You still keep in contact with me and you're my go to for book and music recommendations. You encourage me and support me in your own special way and I am so honored to be able to call you my friend. Love you lots Sars.

To Katie Weisz. It's been two years since I've lived in the same city as you, but you too haven't stopped texting me or checking up on me from time to time. I can't tell you how much that means to me. You've always known how to cheer me up and put a smile on my face and I am so grateful for that and for your friendship. You'll forever and always be my big. I still have my anchor pendent and cherish it so much.

To Jenna Hildabrand. I am so honored to call you a friend. You are so strong and have been such a huge support in my life. Thank you for all you've done for me.

Thank you for continuing to check up on me and to text me and love me in your own special way. I am blessed to have the opportunity to call you friend and a best friend at that.

To Mike Spegele, who was my roommate that became my big brother, thank you for your random texts and phone calls, which brighten my day each time they occur. Even though I've moved from Gainesville and you're incredibly busy you still make it a priority to check up on your little sister to see how she is doing. A part of my heart still resides in Kristen's corner at the intersection of Spegle Street and Webber Way.

To Nicole White, Jackie Schaefer, Katie Sonier, Stephanie Peck, Alina Ayoub and Kim Mockel: Thank you for including me in the best group message ever. We've made countless memories and I hope we make many more. I can never flail with other people like I can flail with you all. Damage control is an honored role and I would do it for any of you in a heartbeat. I love each and every one of you so much. I will always treasure the nickname KFox because with you guys it feels like a title of honor.

To Brianna Peppin. I know I haven't known you for a long time, but I feel like I've known you for much longer. I am so grateful for your friendship and that I have someone to talk to who can relate to how I feel. Never give up in your fight my dear. It's the mental battle that's the hardest, but I know deep down inside you're stronger than any mental army that comes your way. You will defeat it, just don't ever give up.

To Katie Olson. I literally started hanging out with you a month ago, but I feel like we've been friends for much longer. You say that I'm an inspiration to you, but you too are an encouragement to me. I know God has a special plan for you in this life and I am so proud of you for striving to keep on pushing on in life regardless of all the hurdles you've had to face recently. I am honored to call you a friend. Thank you for making an impact on my life and for treating me like me and not letting my medical issues stop you from getting close to me.

To Ashley Franken. Thank you for being such a cheerful and fun-spirited soul. God had a reason for me walking into Office Depot on that cold, dark, stormy night and that reason was so that I could meet you. Thank you for encouraging me and helping me through my days. Any day I get to spend with you is a good day in my book.

To Sherri Alonso. Thank you for sacrificing your time and energy to come out to my house and do Splankna with me. You have such an amazing heart and I know God has innumerable plans for you. He will bless you. You are His precious child and you do all you can to follow His word. I am forever grateful for what you've done for me and the love and care you've shown me.

To Jim Kenaston. It's been nice getting to know you and I enjoy our daily email conversations. Thank you for helping to keep my spirits up and for entertaining me with various youtube videos, comics or jokes. I've learned a lot from you and I appreciate the time you devote to conversing with me!

To Dan Jones. I know I just met you, but you've brought so much joy into my life. You are such a gentleman and treat me with such respect and courtesy. I am honored to be friends for life with you! Thank you for brightening my days, giving me company to hang out with and taking me fun places. I always enjoy being with you, no matter what we are doing. From stalking reptile stores, to feeding giraffes, to enjoying coffee, a movie and other things, each minute I'm with you is a blast!

To Andrea Lorio. You are such a talented photographer. Thank you so much for letting me use your beautiful photo for the cover of my book. Although you may live in Italy and I live in the USA, I'm blessed that you haven't let international borders stop us from getting connected.

To Krishana Kraft: Thank you so much for being my amazing editor. I know there would be countless more errors in my book if it wasn't for your hard work!

To my Florida friends who haven't stopped talking to me just because I left Gainesville-I love you all so much. To my old roommates thank you for still being you and for loving me. This shout out goes to Chris Hogan, Robert Montgomery, Travis Weber, Jenna Demczak,

Lissette Portocarrero, Ashley Hunt and Sara Sada.

To the guys who have become my brothers: Billy Vann, thank you for still calling and texting me to see how I'm doing. Michael Star, thank you for your sweet phone calls and messages that you send my way. To Derek Hunt, my other big brother, who still looks out for me and helps me out with stuff even though we live across the country from each other.

To Dr. Marissa Higgins, Melissa Daigneault, McKinley Carden, Tori Miller & Heather Wing: Thank you guys for never ceasing to show your love and care for me.

To my Virginia friends. Even though I haven't seen you all for years you continue to check up on me and send me love and support. This goes out to you Sheri & Jim Reed, Sofia Herrera, Alice Yu, Lauren Brindley, Cassie Smith, Taylor Crosson, Lauren Boenau,

Jenn Hogan, Dawn Xiang, Carly Salas, Kattie Evans and my entire Companion family. Love you all so much!

To my Colorado friends. Thank you for making me feel loved when I've felt so alone. This shout out goes to you Anna Wolff, Kalie Kirk, Jourdan Squires and Lydia Armstrong.

To a guy who's impacted me in ways many can't, thank you Jared Sylvester for being such a great friend to me and showing me love and care in your own special way.

To Hannah Van Petten: Girl it was a blast when you came down and spent the weekend with me. I can't wait to continue to make memories with you. You're such a smart, caring, fun-loving person and I'm so blessed to have you as a friend.

To Michelle Mendelsohn: You and Mike Barnett are the best. Thank you for making an effort to come visit me when I was in the hospital and for also checking up on me while I was at Mayo. You constantly brighten my day and I am so honored to have you as a friend. I can't wait to make more memories with you and I surely treasure every second I get to spend with you.

I also want to give a shout out to the people I've met recently who've looked past my medical issues and have given me the gift of their friendship. This goes out to you, Abi Spears, Tori Olson, Ryan Pacheco, Chris Bodily and Anthony Shea.

Thank you to the staff at Focus on the Family. I know your constant prayers and support have given me the fuel I need to keep going. Thank you Bill Elfstrom, Jeff Brown, Kyle Adams, Sandy Bove, Beckie Stewart, Gary Booker, John Bethany, Bruce Peppin and Karissa Woods.

To Ketty Kerns. You constantly bring a smile to my lips. From sending me encouraging emails or texts to finding me clothes or other things make me happy you constantly brighten my day. I was blessed the minute God brought you into my life and I continued to be blessed every time I see or talk to you.

To Melinda Debold. Thank you for sharing Lucy Pearl with my family and me. God has such a special plan for you. Continue to trust in Him and find His hope even when everything seems to be going against you. You are stronger than you know.

To those I've met recently on social media. Keep fighting your fight, never give up no matter how hard it gets. God gives us each the strength we need to face our battles so never forget that as you fight. When you feel like there is nothing left for you in this world

push on because you cannot let
this disease ever win.

Made in the USA
Charleston, SC
08 November 2015